IT WORKS

IT WORKS

By Ronald G. Miller

To Ellen 11-9-04

May all your Dreams come true.

Ron Miller

INKWELL PRODUCTIONS
Scottsdale, Arizona

First Printing November, 2003

ISBN: 0-9728118-7-7

LOC: 2003105304

Published by Inkwell Productions
3370 N Hayden Road #123-276
Scottsdale, AZ 85251
Telephone (480) 315-9636
Fax (480)315-9641
Toll free (888) 324-BOOK (2665)
Website: www.inkwellproductions.com
Email: info@inkwellproductions.com

Manufactured in the United States of America

To my three children,
Ronnie, Roger and Karen Miller

I Love You

"We were very pleased with the content and presentation of Mr. Miller's information. His knowledge and enthusiasm helped to make the seminar a success. Those who attended the seminar rated it very highly."

-American Lung Association

"Thank you for taking time out of your busy schedule to speak to our membership. You were well received and rated an outstanding and dynamic speaker."

-Downey Board of Realtors, Inc.

"Your dynamic presentation was received with much enthusiasm from our membership. We only wish we could have spent more time with you."

-Azusa Glendora Board of Realtors

"Thank you for taking the time from your schedule to address our Organization. Your valuable information assists us in helping our clients and enhances our professionalism. Thanks again."

-Realty Investment Association of California

"The Orange County Chapter of the National Association for Professional Saleswomen values the information you shared and would be happy to recommend your name to other groups and organizations as a dynamic speaker".

-National Association for Professional Saleswomen

"You gave us an abundance of new techniques, ideas, and goal setting systems which I feel certain will enhance and add to our daily productivity."

- John Hall and Associates

PREFACE

I put this book together because I know that it can help you. I want to share with you my knowledge of secrets that have been used for hundreds of years by successful people in all walks of life. I hope you dedicate your life to the lessons learned in this book, because I know ...
IT WORKS.

In all of my years of study and experience, I have come to the conclusion that success equals goals, and all else is commentary. It is not possible to realize even a fraction of your potential until you have learned how to set and achieve goals as normally and as naturally as you brush your teeth and comb your hair. While many people have some idea of what they want in life, most have never actually sat down to think about what it would take to get those things and whether or not they are willing to pay the price.

The proper activation and use of your subconscious mind are the most important discoveries you will ever make because they are your keys to happiness, health, prosperity and complete self-expression. The subconscious mind is the foundation of all personal greatness and high achievement. Its activation and utilization can be accomplished through the proper use of hypnosis, self-hypnosis, and visualization.

In this book I have combined self-analysis, positive thinking, goal setting, self-hypnosis, and hypnosis to help you achieve success in all areas of life important to you. This is a working system and does not stop once you put the book down. If you really want to achieve financial success, reduce stress, build family ties, quit smoking, lose weight, or obtain any other goal you have in mind, follow the precepts outlined in this book and you will be well on your way to success. You will learn exercises in this book that you will use every day. YOU MAY ASK, "IS IT WORTH IT?" WHAT YOU SHOULD BE SAYING IS, "AM I WORTH IT?" YOU BET YOU ARE! EVERY PERSON HAS A GOD-GIVEN RIGHT TO SUCCEED.

TABLE OF CONTENTS

INTRODUCTION

How To Use This Book For Effective Goal Setting That Works

SETTING GOALS is a moment-to-moment commitment that, when done well, can create a lifetime of health, happiness and prosperity. In order to set effective goals one must examine one's life, creating a "jumping off point" through self-evaluation and analysis. One should also decide where it is he/she would like to go in each of those areas of life.

So, what makes this process any different from all you may have heard before? With the IT WORKS program self-hypnosis scripts are also incorporated into the goal making process. These scripts are a key element in harmonizing both the conscious and subconscious mind, thereby giving a person's thought process continuity and using that continuity and focus to achieve any set goal.

This book will help you achieve your goals!

After you have gone through the process of self-evaluation, you will determine both your life priorities and how you would like to invest your personal resources to accomplish them. Personal resources include time, thought, money, and "sweat capitol". As you honestly evaluate and execute this process you will be guided to create MY LIFE PLAN. This personal daily routine, which you will use for thirty-one days, will eventually become a lifestyle and a way of being which defines your personal success.

Answer the self-evaluation questions and resource questions honestly so as to create a plan which will really work for you.

The more honest you are about what really matters to you and about how much you are willing to invest to achieve your goals, the more effective the hypnotic scripting and the IT WORKS process will be for you. Take time to really consider each part of the process and invest time in yourself everyday to make it happen... You are worth it!

Use the self-hypnotic scripts to achieve your goals.

After you have completed the evaluation and analysis portion of the book, I will show you how to use self-hypnosis along with daily goal-setting sheets to help you achieve your goals ... IT WORKS!

SECTION ONE:
Mind Power and Goal Setting

Whatever the mind of man can conceive,
and believe, it can achieve.

– Napoleon Hill

Ronald G. Miller

CHAPTER 1

HYPNOSIS AND YOUR SUBCONSCIOUS

Imagination is latent in your mind this very moment. It has the power to make you whoever your mind sees and your heart feels you to be.

The human mind is like an onion with many layers. The outer layer is our conscious mind, which helps with our daily decision-making process and works according to the reality principle. It is intelligent, realistic, logical and proactive, especially in new situations where we have to apply rational thought processes to work out what to do and how to do it. However, it can only deal with between five and nine things at any time and is easily overloaded.

The subconscious or hidden layer of the onion works on 'auto pilot', reacting according to the pleasure principle. It seeks to avoid pain and obtain pleasure and survival regardless of external considerations. It is concerned with our emotions, imagination, and memories as well as our autonomic nervous system, which automatically controls our internal organs. These main functions are closely interlinked. The mind affects the body and the body affects the mind. The subconscious is powerful and clever at dealing with multiple complex instructions at one time but is not 'intelligent'.

The key to health, happiness and prosperity has been found in the subconscious mind. When your subconscious mind is used correctly you will be able to solve any problem, overcome any obstacle, and achieve any goal you sincerely desire.

All personal greatness and individual achievement are based on how the subconscious mind is used. Whenever you have been wrestling with a problem and have suddenly come up with a great idea that turned out to be the perfect solution, you were tapping into your subconscious mind. Once you begin using your subconscious capabilities in a systematic way, you will get ideas seemingly from 'out of the blue'. Because of childhood conditioning we tend to ignore our own ideas, assuming that they could not be worth very much, when, in fact, they could change our lives.

Your subconscious mind responds best to clear, firm affirmations. You will also find that when you stop vacillating and make a firm, clear decision that you are going to do something no matter the cost, everything suddenly starts to work in your favor. Make the decision that you are going to do whatever it takes to achieve your goal, and nothing will stop you. Your main job is to keep your thoughts on your goal. Your mind will automatically and continuously solve each problem on the way to your goal and when the problem arises you can trust absolutely in this subconscious power to function for you as long as your goal is clear. Any kind of negativity, anger, worry, or impatience diminishes your power and clouds your thinking. Destructive emotions of any kind interfere with the calm, positive attitude your subconscious requires for optimal functioning.

A characteristic of successful men and women is that they never use the word "failure". They look upon temporary defeats and setbacks as simply another way of learning how to succeed.

They seek within every obstacle or disappointment the seed of an equal or greater benefit or opportunity. They learn from every experience. They refuse to get upset. They keep their minds calm, positive, and focused on their goals.

Think about your goals all the time.

Your subconscious mind operates best under two conditions. The first is when your conscious mind is concentrating 100 % on a specific problem or goal. The second is when your conscious mind is busy with something else altogether. Following is a five-step process to bring all the powers of your subconscious mind to bear on a single issue.

Step One: Define the problem or goal clearly.
Step Two: Gather as much information as you can.
Step Three: Consciously try to solve the problem by reviewing all information.
Step Four: Turn it over to your subconscious mind confidently.
Step Five: Get your conscious mind busy elsewhere.

When the answer comes, you must act upon it immediately. If you get the urge to telephone someone or to say something or do something, and it feels exactly right, act in faith and follow your instincts. The Law of Subconscious Activity states, " Any thought, plan, goal, or idea held continuously in your conscious mind must be brought into reality by your subconscious mind, whether positive or negative." Sometimes you will get an urge to buy a book or magazine or you will open one to the exact page that has the answer that you need. This will happen more frequently the more you trust your subconscious mind.

You are always free to choose the kind of world that you wish to live in. And you do choose it every day by the thoughts you think. Many people find that daydreaming or relaxing on a park bench triggers subconscious activity. You might also choose to listen to classical music, go for a walk or commune with nature. The sounds of the ocean on the seashore seem to have a powerful impact on the subconscious, as do those of any natural running water. Any form of deep relaxation or meditation also stimulates your subconscious mind.

A subconscious solution will come to you from one of three sources. The first is intuition. Trust your intuition. The second is chance encounters with people or information. Often these will be strangers met while traveling or in social situations. The third source is unpredictable events. Successful, happy people make a habit of searching even the most difficult situation for something positive, something they can learn or some way in which they can benefit.

WHAT IS HYPNOSIS?

Hypnosis is a natural state. In the course of life every individual is regularly in this state; when falling asleep or upon first waking, or while gazing distractedly at nothing.

The best way to view hypnosis is as a state of intense relaxation and concentration in which the mind becomes remote and detached from everyday cares and concerns. In this relaxed state the subconscious part of the mind is best able to respond creatively to suggestion and imagery. It can focus on change and on the ways to do so, free from analytical or anxious thoughts.

In hypnosis one is neither asleep nor unconscious, but in an altered or alternative state of consciousness in which one 'lets things happen' through the subconscious mind rather than trying to make them happen with the conscious mind. Because one is deeply relaxed, the suggestions given by the hypnotist will be carried out when one comes out of the hypnotic state.

SELF-HYPNOSIS

It has been maintained that all hypnosis is essentially self-hypnosis. It is certainly impossible to be hypnotized by someone else unless you want or allow it to happen. Self-hypnosis is a way of safely bypassing the conscious mind and should only be practiced on the advice of a professional therapist. But once you have learned how to hypnotize yourself, practice will enable you to put yourself in that state whenever you wish to, quickly and easily. Psychotic and severely mentally unstable people, however, should never attempt self-hypnosis.

Can Anyone Be Hypnotized?

Anyone who wishes to be can be, with the possible exceptions of babies and the mentally challenged, since they do not know what the hypnotist is attempting to do and can not concentrate upon his voice. I believe anyone can be helped through hypnosis. Factors such as motivation, personal rapport between therapist and subject, and physical surroundings contribute to or detract from hypnotizability.

Does Self- Hypnosis Work Just as Well as Hypnosis?

Yes. And sometimes even better. An important aspect of self-hypnosis is that, once learned, the skill is with you twenty-four hours a day wherever you happen to be. Some people with serious problems like addiction to drugs or alcohol need an instructor to set up a suitable program for them. Once this is established, self-hypnosis is carried on by the subject in real-life situations on a day-to-day basis. The role of the hypnotist is that of a teacher, activating and developing what is already inside the person rather than, as may have been supposed, imposing suggestions from the outside.

FACTS ABOUT HYPNOSIS

Self-hypnosis is one of the great keys to health and happiness.

When fully relaxed the body and mind can achieve optimum performance.

There are no side effects of hypnosis.

The hypnotic trance is not sleep. Hypnosis is more closely associated with meditation.

Intelligence and will power are no obstacles. In fact, those qualities add to one's ability to be hypnotized.

In hypnosis, the conscious mind, the ego, is suppressed, and the individual's natural instinct, his subconscious, is fully exposed.

Hypnosis allows the mind to focus and give full concentration to a specific task or function that would be impossible in the normal waking state.

Under hypnosis, you will neither be in a trance nor will you be unconscious. You will hear everything that is going on around you. Once you reawaken, you will remember everything in detail.

Many people wonder, 'Am I sure to wake up from hypnosis?' The answer is 'Yes'. Even if the hypnotist left you in a state of hypnosis, that state would automatically be transformed to sleep and you would reawaken after having slept your fill.

What happens when a hypnotized subject is told to perform an act that conflicts with his moral code of behavior? He may: 1) Not respond at all, but sometimes state his reason for not responding. 2) Become agitated or excited and may start to cry. 3) Break the trance, forcing himself into consciousness.

No one can be made to do anything against one's usual moral standards while under hypnosis.

A few of the ways hypnosis has been used to help people are:

Acne
Alchoholism
Allergies
Amnesia
Anesthesia
Anorexia
Anxiety
Arthritis
Asthma
Bladder Control
Bronchitis
Bulimia
Claustrophobia
Compulsions
Concentration
Confidence
Depression
Dieting/ Losing Weight
Drug Dependency
Emphysema
Energy
Fear
Frigidity
Habits
Headaches
Heartburn
Hiccups
Hypochondria
Impotence
Inferiority Complex
Inhibitions
Insecurity
Learning Habits
Memory
Migrane
Headaches
Money Making
Motion Sickness
Motivation
Nail Biting
Nightmares
Obsessions
Organization
Orgasms/ Sexual Problems
Phobias
Poise
Posture
Procrastination
Reading Skills
Salesmanship
Shyness
Sleeping
Smoking
Snoring
Stress
Stuttering
Temper Tantrums
Tension
Toothaches/ Pain Control
Twitching
Warts
Yawning

CHAPTER 2

POSITIVE THINKING

Every day in every way I am better and better.

Before delving into self-evaluation let us discuss some common obstacles to effective goal setting.

THE SEVEN MAJOR NEGATIVE EMOTIONS

1. Fear
2. Jealousy
3. Hatred
4. Revenge
5. Greed
6. Superstition
7. Anger

THE SIX BASIC FEARS

1. Fear of poverty.
2. Fear of criticism.
3. Fear of ill health.
4. Fear of loss of love.
5. Fear of old age.
6. Fear of death.

FIFTY-FOUR FAMOUS ALIBIS

1. If I didn't have a wife and family ...
2. If I had enough "pull"...
3. If I had money ...
4. If I had a good education...
5. If I could get a job...
6. If I had good health...
7. If I only had time...
8. If times were better...
9. If other people understood me...
10. If conditions around me were only different...
11. If I could live my life over again...
12. If I did not fear what "they" would say...
13. If I had been given a chance...
14. If other people didn't "have it in for me"...
15. If nothing happens to stop me...
16. If I were only younger...
17. If I could only do what I want...
18. If I had been born rich...
19. If I could get to meet "the right people"...
20. If I had the talent some people have...
21. If I dared to assert myself...
22. If I only had embraced past opportunities...
23. If people didn't get on my nerves...
24. If I didn't have to keep house and look after children...
25. If I could save some money...
26. If the boss only appreciated me...
27. If only I had somebody to help me...
28. If my family understood me...
29. If I lived in a big city...

30. If I could just get started…
31. If I were only free…
32. If I had the personality of some people…
33. If I were not so fat…
34. If my talents were known…
35. If I could just get a "break"…
36. If I could only get out of debt…
37. If I hadn't failed…
38. If I only knew how…
39. If everybody didn't oppose me…
40. If I didn't have so many worries…
41. If I could marry the right person…
42. If people weren't so dumb…
43. If my family were not so extravagant…
44. If I were sure of myself…
45. If luck were not against me…
46. If I had not been born under the wrong star…
47. If it were not true that "what is to be will be"…
48. If I didn't have to work so hard…
49. If I hadn't lost my money…
50. If I lived in a different neighborhood…
51. If I didn't have a "past"…
52. If I only had a business of my own…
53. If other people would listen to me…
54. If I had the courage to see myself as I really am, I would find out what is wrong with me, and correct it…

THIRTY OBSTACLES TO SUCCESS

1. Unfavorable hereditary background
2. Lack of a well defined purpose in life
3. Lack of ambition to aim above mediocrity
4. Insufficient education
5. Lack of self-discipline
6. Ill health
7. Unfavorable environmental influences during childhood
8. Procrastination
9. Lack of persistence
10. Negative personality
11. Lack of controlled sexual urge
12. Uncontrolled desire for "something for nothing"
13. Lack of a well defined power of decision
14. One or more of the six basic fears
15. Wrong selection of mate in marriage
16. Over-caution
17. Wrong selection of associates in business
18. Superstition and prejudice
19. Wrong selection of vocation
20. The habit of indiscriminate spending
21. Lack of enthusiasm
22. Intolerance
23. Intemperance
24. Inability to cooperate with others
25. Possession of power that was not acquired through self-effort
26. Intentional dishonesty
27. Egotism and vanity
28. Guessing instead of thinking
29. Lack of capital

30. Lack of a well-defined plan of action.

Start off each morning by saying a positive affirmation. When you affirm positively, visualize clearly and believe absolutely, you will be led irresistibly to do and say the right thing at the right time. You unlock your full potential for health, happiness and prosperity.

We have all heard of or lived some of these obstacles. Can you turn them around? Of course you can. You need to get into the habit of thinking and living positively. This book will help you to do so.

Listed below are some of the misconceptions about success.

I cannot be successful because I do not have the right background, or enough education or money.

Although these assets are helpful, they are not assurance of success. It is a matter of wanting to succeed and then doing what is necessary. I come from a very poor Maine family. Most people in Maine near whom I lived were poor, but we were at the bottom of the totem pole. I can remember when I was a little child Mom shot a porcupine with an old shotgun. The recoil knocked her down, but she got up, dusted herself off, and we ate a good meal that night. My early childhood taught me the value of money and has helped me immensely in my quest for financial independence. In my senior year I dropped out of high school and joined the Marines. Education was not pushed as much as getting a job in our home. I did finish high school and college in the Marine Corps, but I do not know how much college actually helped me to achieve success. It did teach me discipline. College is also important depending upon in which field you have chosen your goal. I took a lot of courses including Dale Carnegie and I loved to read, so I read everything I could get my hands on. Anyone who really believes he can, can achieve success. One's background does not hold one back. It's what one does today and tomorrow that counts.

One must work many hours to be successful.

It is not so much a matter of the amount of time you spend working towards your success, but what you do with that time. It only takes a slight edge to be successful. Most people coast along from problem to problem. They don't realize that they only need to apply a little extra effort to put them above the norm, and then have smoother sailing. Take that half hour a day spent watching TV and use it to better yourself. Read positive books, meditate, study, or do whatever it takes to get you ahead. And GET ORGANIZED! That was primary to my working less and achieving more. There are a lot of good books and workshops out there to help you. I also use lists. I make a to-do list each night with priorities on the left side. As I work my to-do list, I scratch off each item. Any item left at the end of the day is added to my next day's list. This works for me. Remember, work smart not hard.

It takes a lot of luck to be successful.

It does take some "luck" to be successful. However, it takes more hard work, diligence and determination to make success happen. I once heard a successful business owner say that he spelled luck W-O-R-K. I admit that I have been lucky in life. On the other hand, I was also open to and aware of opportunities. When I was buying real estate in the 1960's everyone told me I was crazy. They didn't think so in the 1970's when property values skyrocketed. You must analyze all situational facts, and if 'it' looks right, go for it!

Successful people do not make mistakes.

Successful people do make mistakes HOWEVER they learn from them and make sure they do not repeat them. One of the first houses that I bought was gutted. The frame was still good. I didn't know anything about rebuilding a house, but some Marines and I gave it a good shot. I make a lot of mistakes. I put bathroom tiles around the tub and then tried to put the tub in. Wrong. I had to pull the bathroom tile back off and put the tub in first. I initially put the bathroom door on upside down and backwards so one had to open the door and go around it to turn the light on. The doorknob was so low one almost had to stoop to open it. Probably the biggest blooper that effected that poor house was the water heater. I installed new carpet, then put in the hot water heater and turned it on. That was back when the hot water heater was in the closet. I returned the next morning to find the valve had popped and there was an inch of water all over my new carpet. I had to take out the carpet and stretch it on a rack to dry. I learned A LOT from that old house. Everyone makes mistakes. You must choose to learn from them and go forward.

It is only success if one makes a lot of money or receives public recognition for one's work.

Although there are benefits to financial prosperity and public praise, it is the accomplishment of self-fulfillment which is a true attribute of success. And no one may know about that but you. I volunteered for a church suicide hot line for several years at the same time I was running a financial planning firm. Since the hotline required manning 24 hours a day, I sometimes went there late at night. I believe that I gave comfort to a lot of people, but the only people who knew I was doing this were my wife, the people who worked with me on the hotline, and perhaps a few more. I believe that I was helped a lot more than the people who called me. That experience opened my eyes to a lot that I had never thought about before.

If one had help along the way, it is not true success.

Success rarely happens alone. People who are successful often create a Mastermind Group whom they directly recognize and credit when they have finally accomplished their particular goals. Think of "All the people I would like to thank for making my dream happen..." Setting up a Mastermind Group works. I used it in my companies and found that people working together come up with some fantastic ideas. Two or more people with a common goal are all it takes. Set consistent meetings and work an agenda that moves you towards your goal. Hang out with people who are already successful. Some of it will rub off.

Success is a goal.

Success is a journey not a destination. It is more than what you achieve or get for yourself. It is what you get from the experience of doing it. Saying you "want to be a success" leaves one asking "At what?" Most people, myself included, find life anticlimactic once goals have been achieved. The 'getting there' should be the fun. Once you achieve your goal, you will find yourself looking around asking, "What's next?" Achieving a goal is satisfying, but it still leaves one with the question, "Is that all?"

Once I am successful my troubles are over.

Success may change your circumstances but you are still human. Life will still have its ups and downs. Enjoy your success. Enjoy the moment and create your life as a work-in-progress. Problems arise no matter how many goals are achieved. How we handle our problems is what makes all the difference in the world. Because I had a lot of property for 25 years people seemed to assume I had a lot of money. What I really had, at least initially, was a lot of negative cash flow. People frequently asked me for money for whatever pet project they had going or just because they wanted it. They assumed I had more than I needed. That was not the case. I remember wanting to buy a Rolls Royce until someone who owned one told me that people keyed the side of the car and did other damage to it just because. We all have problems, rich or poor. Most of them can be overcome. A lot depends upon attitude.

Know your enemy.

What is the enemy of your goal setting and resultant success? Let us discuss common culprits.

Procrastination

Putting off the details of achieving your goal can be deadly to success. Train yourself to finish what you start. To keep yourself from becoming scattered, focus on one task at a time until it is accomplished. We all have a tendency to procrastinate. Handle the tough, unpleasant problems first. Create your first list of priorities and do them. You can train yourself not to procrastinate.

Fear of Leaving Comfort Zone

One must remember that a comfort zone is only comfortable because it is what is known. If what you know and the life you have is not what you desire, however, a change must be made. And doing something different is, for most people, very uncomfortable. Great things can happen for you when you embrace your Discomfort Zone. Charles Dubois once said, "We must be prepared, at any moment, to sacrifice who we are for who we are capable of becoming." A friend, Rich, and I do what we call 'getting out of the box'. We make a point to do different things, eat at new places, sit in a different location at church, and many other 'out of the box' activities. Once you take the first step of leaving your comfort zone, the ensuing path becomes easier to traverse. I like to do this because I always learn more.

In Phoenix, we have a downtown art walk. Part of the area is kind of rough, consisting of struggling young artists who work out of their homes, lofts, warehouses, or wherever they can set up. The first Friday evening of each month, the city provides shuttle buses to about 40 different locations open to the public. Many of the places have music, food, and great art displayed for sale. The first time I tried this I was a bit nervous. It was dark and I was downtown in South Phoenix. I had a lot of fun and learned a lot. South Phoenix is quite nice in most areas and the young artists are very good. When you start a new venture or set your goals, you are out of your comfort zone. If you push forward, you will find being out becomes increasingly easy.

Self-Limiting Thinking

What one thinks, one becomes. Success manuals are replete with quotes about this subject. If you think you can't, you are right. If you think you can, you are right. You can change a habit by catching yourself before or during engaging in the habit you are trying to change. You can stop self-limiting thinking the same way. When you think that you can't do something, stop right there and visualize yourself doing it. This takes a while, but it works! When I was a young Marine, I swore profusely. While I didn't like it, I also did not know how to stop. The words just seemed to pop out. I finally discovered that if I stopped every time I started to swear and changed to a different word, I could stop swearing. It took about a month, but I did it. The same system works with an "I can't" attitude.

Allowing the Past or future to Effect your Present

Live in the present moment. When you allow the fears of your past or the worries of your future to contaminate your present moment, you make yourself less effective in achieving the results that you desire. Have you ever given yourself a quiet moment? Most people live in the future or the past. They never stop to see what is happening right now. They tend to worry about what is going to happen tomorrow, or what they did last week. If you concentrate on the moment and what you are doing right now, you don't have time to worry about next week and you can do a better, more efficient job right now.

Fear of Failure

What appears to be failure happens. It is a part of the learning process. It is what you do with that knowledge and experience that commands the course of your destiny. Everyone has some fear of 'What if I fail, what will people think of me?' Much of this type of thinking can be overcome by working and living in the moment. I once read that you should consider the very worst that can happen to you, look at it, and go forward. Thinking that way results in more calm. Analyze any new venture or large goal before you start it. This helps you take away the fear of failure.

Allowing your mood to control you instead of controlling your mood

Good things happen to good people. Happy things happen to happy people. Happiness is your birthright, so do not settle for less. Commit yourself to joy. C.S. Lewis once said, "Joy is the serious business of heaven." Have you ever noticed how some people are always moody or grumpy? That is a choice. Who knows why they are that way? I know that I don't like being around that type of person and I believe most people feel the same way. You can choose to be moody or upbeat and positive. That isn't to say that you have to be positive all the time. Everyone gets down sometimes. It's how long you allow yourself to stay down that matters. A while back a gentleman who was usually down worked in one of my Las Vegas offices. I received so many complaints from other people in the office that I finally had to let him go. Your moods are your choice and may determine your outcomes.

Creating unrealistic goals

It is important to create goals which incorporate the 'human element'. Goals which do not allow for rest and recreation, do not make allowances for insufficient information or the influences of other people in the process, or which only factor in best performance and do not allow for the backsliding inevitable in life are unrealistic goals. As a general rule, this form of goal setting does not tend to be the problem. If anything, it seems to be the opposite. People's goals are too low. On the other hand, if you are making $100,000 now and your situation isn't about to change a lot, you can't expect to make $1,000,000 next year. You need to make realistic goals based on what you are doing now and what you are willing to do in the future to achieve them.

Not Dreaming BIG Enough

It is not effective to set goals which do not present a challenge. It is more impressive for a batter to get fewer home runs in the big league than to stay in the minors and be the home run champion. If you are not prepared to stretch yourself and work hard, you are extremely unlikely to accomplish anything of real worth. Goal setting is not initially easy, but it does become less taxing as you practice it regularly. Once you set goals consistently and have worked a goal system for a period of time, it becomes a habit. You need to think big and challenge yourself. If you set a goal and don't make it 100% you are closer than if you hadn't tried at all. Don't beat yourself up over it. Reset your goals and move on.

Giving Up

Never ever, ever, ever, give up! Many times on the success journey people are frustrated by setbacks. Remember, success could be just around the corner. The only way to know for sure and to get there is to Never Give Up! This is where the rubber meets the road. Some people give up because they are frustrated. Most successful people are so today because, no matter what happened, they never gave up. Persistence alone can be omnipotent.

Now that we have discussed some of the pitfalls to goal setting let's discuss some effective ways to overcome those obstacles and achieve our goals. Positive thinking is a powerful tool for surpassing obstacles and achieving success.

THE SEVEN MAJOR POSITIVE EMOTIONS
1. Desire
2. Faith
3. Love
4. Sex
5. Enthusiasm
6. Romance
7. Hope

I first started setting goals after reading Napoleon Hill's *Think and Grow Rich*. I was a married Marine and my wife was pregnant with our second son. It was 1963 and we were making under $200 per month gross income while living in substandard government housing on 32nd Street in San Diego. We were making payments on our eight-year-old car and though that was the only bill we had, we were dead broke at the end of each month. Because we could go to the movies at the military base for ten cents each, my buddy and I used to go down the side of the road and pick up beer bottles to turn in at two cents each!

One day I simply had to have the carburetor fixed, so I took the car to a nearby mechanic. Since I had just had my taxes done and knew I would be refunded $149, I told the mechanic I would pay him from my tax return. My IRS check was $156 and my bill from the mechanic was $43. I took the check over to the garage and he cashed it, taking out his $43. I went back home with $113 in my pocket and boy was I happy. A bubble of excitement welled up inside me. The four of us could go out to eat and buy some items for the baby! As we prepared to go, there was a knock on my door. The taxman had figured my taxes wrong and it turned out that I owed $156. The mechanic and I had overlooked this earlier that day in our excitement to get the repair bill settled.

I didn't have $5, let alone $156. I felt like someone had just punched me in the stomach. I went to Navy relief for assistance. They helped me by fronting me the money and I paid them back $10 a month for almost a year and a half.

That was when I picked up *Think and Grow Rich* by Napoleon Hill.

By 1965, having set goals and applied his principles, I had purchased my first house. I used money borrowed from my in-laws. Though still in the Marines I began working nights for a local real estate company and attending a local college. I also began buying houses from veterans. When a veteran was transferred I took over his mortgage, usually with no down payment. The house was worth basically what he paid for it in the first place due to lack of appreciation. While my payments were under $100 per month my rent was less than that, so I had a large negative cash flow. By this time I owned several properties so I started a TV shop out of my garage to help pay for the negative cash flow. I hired people from the base to come out nights and repair televisions. Days I worked for the Marines. Nights and weekends I went to school, delivered TV's, studied, listed, bought, and sold real estate. I was fairly busy!

In 1978 I retired from the Marines, became a real estate broker, and opened my own company. I worked with a financial planning firm and a tax and accounting company. Eventually, I bought out the tax and accounting company and opened a mortgage company and a financial planning company. I now had eight companies, four in California and four in Nevada. I also presented financial planning, real estate, and goal setting seminars nationwide. I accomplished all of this by setting goals. If you set goals and believe that you will achieve them you most likely will.

Release the imprisoned possibilities within you.

You can release imprisoned possibilities within your imagination through positive thinking. I once heard a story which really moved me. It illustrates this point well. A polio victim paralyzed from the neck down and restricted by an iron lung sought the freedom of independent breath.

As a boy in Tennessee he and other children had pretended to breathe like tree frogs. They took in air with their tongues, forcing it down their windpipes. When they exhaled their lungs deflated like balloons.

Having been in bed for six years with polio, the man recalled this play. By incorporating 'tree frog breathing' he was able to find freedom and independence from the iron lung and his bed. And what did he do with his newfound freedom? He became an attorney. His wife drove him to school and wheeled him into class at the University of San Diego. Here, taking notes was his first obstacle. He couldn't take notes conventionally; writing with his teeth was not efficient enough for note-taking, and a tape recorder was too awkward, He simply listened and remembered.

He was then told that he had diabetes. No sooner had he gotten that under control than his doctor informed him he had an ulcer. A mysteriously high fever (reaction to the medications he was taking) raged in his body for a year. Still, he graduated with his diploma and passed the bar exam. He went on to practice law!

Some obstacles remained. His face reddened if he talked too long in court. This was really nothing to worry about. A cold however, would be something to worry about because it could be fatal. However, asked how he deals with colds he replies, " I don't get colds."

Asked about the fact that if he falls asleep or faints while he is out on his own and no one is around who knows about his condition and can give him rescue breathing, he would die, he replies, "I try to think about that as little as possible."

You too can use your imagination to think of ways in which you can harness your handicap, profit from your problem, capitalize on your crisis, and even make your sorrow serve you.

Direct your imagination to work for you in the art of getting along with people as well. To succeed in the field of human relations, bring out the strengths of your personality with your imagination. Use visualization to see yourself as you would like others to see you. When you walk into the room are you relaxed, confident, smiling, and full of positive energy? The more you firmly hold that image of yourself in your mind the more certain it is that you will become this person. The opposite is also true. If your mind holds a picture of you being "stressed out" and "losing it" by being irritable, sensitive, and touchy, that is precisely the way you will react and you will fail miserably in the school of human relations. Your imagination has the power to transform and recreate your personality!

See in your mind's-eye who you want to be and become it.

Thoughts are powerful. Our thoughts are the seeds of our dreams. They begin the process of making things happen. The way we perceive ourselves directly affects the results we experience. A young boy was inspired one day when he heard a man who spoke at his school. The man said, "Who knows if there is an Olympic Champion somewhere in this auditorium today? If you think you can, you can. If you believe something strongly enough, you can make it happen in your life." That young man decided that day that he wanted to be an Olympic Champion more than anything else in the world. Years later, in Berlin, Germany, that boy, Jesse Owens, realized his dream with 4 gold medals. Through training, hard work, and a single vision he transformed from a small Negro boy with spindly legs (in a time long before the Civil rights movement) to one of the greatest athletes who ever lived.

Use your mind to become who *you* really *want* to be.

There was a man who worked in a lime quarry for almost a decade. One day he came to the conclusion that his life was 'a waste' and that it was time for him to get busy and do something about it. That night he went home and announced to his wife that he was going to become a lawyer. He resumed his education and eventually enrolled at the state university. Because he continued to work at the quarry full-time while he went to school, he usually only had thirty minutes to study. Yet, with the help of his wife and kids, he achieved his goal. "Just because I worked in a quarry for many years is no reason I can't be a lawyer," he decided. "You can do a lot of studying in thirty minutes when you have to."

Transform your physical appearance through positive thinking.

A positive attitude and positive self-image radiates from you through twinkling eyes, a beaming smile, and a radiant personality. Hold that picture in your mind and you will become that person. If you think of yourself as dull and unattractive, you project that feeling to others and your glum appearance will make you less attractive.

Your mind can also help you lose weight. Keep a picture in your mind of how you would like to look. When temptation strikes with visions of chocolate cream pie, tell your mind to think about what that pie will do to your goal. The self-hypnotic script for weight loss contained later in the book will assist you with goals of this type.

It is easy to understand how using the subconscious mind works. When you create a clear mental picture and get a sharp mental definition of what you really want, you become excited. Excitement becomes motivation. This motivation moves you to plan, use your imagination, and give action to your inspiration, taking the steps to make things happen for yourself!

THE BOTTOM LINE

FACE IT. Nobody owes you a living.
What you achieve or fail to achieve in your lifetime
is directly related to what you do or fail to do.
No one chooses his parents or his childhood
But you can choose your own direction.
Everyone has problems and obstacles to overcome
But that too is relative to each individual.
NOTHING IS CARVED IN STONE.
You can change anything in your life,
If you want to badly enough.
Excuses are for losers:
Those who take responsibility for their actions
Are the real winners in life.
Winners meet life's challenges head on,
Knowing there are no guarantees,
And they give it all they've got.
And never think it is too late or too early to begin,
Time plays no favorites
And will pass whether you act or not.
TAKE CONTROL OF YOUR LIFE.
Dare to dream and take risks…
Compete.
If you aren't willing to work for your goals
Don't expect others to.
BELIEVE IN YOURSELF!

ATTITUDE

The longer I live, the more I realize the impact of attitude on life. Attitude to me is more important than the past, than education, than money, than circumstances, than failures, than successes, than what other people think or say or do. It is more important than appearance, giftedness or skill. It will make or break a company, a church, a home. The remarkable thing is that we have a choice every day regarding the attitude we will embrace for that day. We cannot change past …we cannot change the fact that people will act a certain way. We cannot change the inevitable. The only thing we can do is play on the one string we have, and that is our attitude. I am convinced that life is 10% what happens to me and 90% how I react to it. And so it is with you … We are all in charge of our Attitude.

- Charles Swindoll

THE MAN WHO THINKS HE CAN

If you think that you are beaten, you are,
If you think you dare not, you don't.
If you like to win, but think you can't,
It is almost certain you won't.

If you think you'll lose, you're lost,
For out in the world we find,
Success begins with a fellow's will,
It's all a state of mind.

If you think you are outclassed, you are,
You've got to think high to rise,
You've got to be sure of yourself before
You can ever win a prize.

Life's battles don't always go
To the stronger or faster man,
But soon or late the man who wins
Is the man **WHO THINKS HE CAN!**

SECTION TWO:
The Process of Goal Setting

A goal is a dream with a date on it.

CHAPTER 3

SELF-EVALUATION AND ANALYSIS

Know Thyself

Now it is time for the self-evaluation portion of this process. As you work through the ensuing pages you will gather information about your goals. You will then use this information to delve further into the technique of effective goal setting.

Self Evaluation

Goal setting done effectively can yield strong results in all areas of life. By setting a variety of goals you incorporate a vision with the motivation to make it happen. Set sharp, clearly-defined short-term, medium-term, and long-term goals. Measure and take pride in the achievement of those goals. You will see results where before it only seemed like wasted effort.

The first step in setting personal goals is to dream. Dream of everything you have always wanted in every facet of your life. There are no limits. Considering what you want to achieve in your lifetime and setting those lifetime goals will provide perspective to shape the following areas:

- Financial and Career
- Family and Friends
- Physical and Health
- Mental and Educational

- Spiritual and Ethical
- Social and Cultural
- Emotional

Self Analysis is a valuable tool to discover who we are and why we act in the ways we do. Learning more about ourselves is the first step to understanding our strengths and weaknesses and how to overcome things in our lives which keep us from achieving our goals.

By thoroughly examining these target areas we can further define which goals are important to us and how we can achieve them.

What would you attempt to do in the preceding areas of your life if you were assured that you would not fail? What would you want from your life if you were certain you could accomplish it? By allowing yourself to dream as you did when a child you allow your imagination to run wild! As you brainstorm, write your ideas so you may later decide which are most important to you. This will assist you in finding and prioritizing your goals in each area.

Please take time now to fill out the following self-evaluation inventory. In addition to the self-evaluation forms located in this book, I highly recommend working with the Myers-Briggs™ Personality evaluation.

SELF-EVALUATION INVENTORY
Financial and Career Area

Respond to each item below by placing an "X" in the box which best expresses the accuracy of each statement as the description of you and your habits. If the statement is not like you at all, check box number one. If it fits you perfectly, check box number seven. The boxes in between allow you to indicate varying degrees of fit.

When you have checked all items, review your ratings and indicate in the box labeled "plus or minus" whether you are satisfied with your honest rating of yourself. Enter a plus (+) if you are pleased with your rating or a minus (-) if you feel a need for a change. The "minus signs" you enter may become suggestions for concrete goal setting in this area.

1 = poor description, 7 = perfect description

	1	**2**	**3**	**4**	**5**	**6**	**7**	**+ or -**
1. I give proper emphasis to financial development in my life.	☐	☐	☐	☐	☐	☐	☐	☐
2. I handle my financial affairs with maturity.	☐	☐	☐	☐	☐	☐	☐	☐
3. I make plans for my financial future.	☐	☐	☐	☐	☐	☐	☐	☐
4. My family uses a family budget.	☐	☐	☐	☐	☐	☐	☐	☐
5. I tend to spend money impulsively.	☐	☐	☐	☐	☐	☐	☐	☐
6. I save a part of my income regularly.	☐	☐	☐	☐	☐	☐	☐	☐
7. I earn about as much as the average person my age.	☐	☐	☐	☐	☐	☐	☐	☐
8. My earnings have increased progressively each year for the last five years.	☐	☐	☐	☐	☐	☐	☐	☐
9. I live within my income.	☐	☐	☐	☐	☐	☐	☐	☐
10. I have a good credit rating.	☐	☐	☐	☐	☐	☐	☐	☐
11. The emphasis I place on making money is properly balanced with the importance of other goals in life.	☐	☐	☐	☐	☐	☐	☐	☐

	1	2	3	4	5	6	7	+ or -
12. I am well prpared to earn a good living.	☐	☐	☐	☐	☐	☐	☐	☐
13. I have used good judgement in my vocational choice.	☐	☐	☐	☐	☐	☐	☐	☐
14. My financial plan provides for a well-balanced life including necessities as well as recreation and entertainment.	☐	☐	☐	☐	☐	☐	☐	☐
15. I expect to be wealthy some day.	☐	☐	☐	☐	☐	☐	☐	☐
16. I manage my money well.	☐	☐	☐	☐	☐	☐	☐	☐
17. I have specific financial goals.	☐	☐	☐	☐	☐	☐	☐	☐
18. I have a workable plan for retirement.	☐	☐	☐	☐	☐	☐	☐	☐
19. I have made satisfactory progress in my career.	☐	☐	☐	☐	☐	☐	☐	☐
20. I have specific plans for further advancement in my career.	☐	☐	☐	☐	☐	☐	☐	☐
21. I have a current will.	☐	☐	☐	☐	☐	☐	☐	☐
22. I regularly invest part of my savings.	☐	☐	☐	☐	☐	☐	☐	☐

SELF-EVALUATION INVENTORY
Physical and Health

Respond to each item below by placing an "X" in the box that best expresses the accuracy of each statement as the description of you and your habits. If the statement is not like you at all, check box number one. If it fits you perfectly, check box number seven. The boxes in between allow you to indicate varying degrees of fit.

When you have checked all items, review your ratings and indicate in the box labeled "plus or minus" whether you are satisfied with your honest rating of yourself. Enter a plus (+) if you are pleased with your rating or a minus (-) if you feel a need for a change. The "minus signs" you enter may become suggestions for concrete goal setting in this area.

1 = poor description, 7 = perfect description

	1	2	3	4	5	6	7	+ or -
1. I eat a balanced diet.	☐	☐	☐	☐	☐	☐	☐	☐
2. My weight is about right.	☐	☐	☐	☐	☐	☐	☐	☐
3. I have an adequate regular exercise program.	☐	☐	☐	☐	☐	☐	☐	☐
4. I get enough rest.	☐	☐	☐	☐	☐	☐	☐	☐
5. I sleep well at night.	☐	☐	☐	☐	☐	☐	☐	☐
6. I often suffer tension in my work.	☐	☐	☐	☐	☐	☐	☐	☐
7. I frequently suffer tension in my family or social life.	☐	☐	☐	☐	☐	☐	☐	☐
8. I have a physical checkup every year.	☐	☐	☐	☐	☐	☐	☐	☐
9. I am often sick.	☐	☐	☐	☐	☐	☐	☐	☐
10. I have plenty of energy.	☐	☐	☐	☐	☐	☐	☐	☐
11. I frequently have indigestion.	☐	☐	☐	☐	☐	☐	☐	☐
12. I am physically stronger than the average person my age.	☐	☐	☐	☐	☐	☐	☐	☐

	1	2	3	4	5	6	7	+ or -
13. I pay little attention to physical development.	☐	☐	☐	☐	☐	☐	☐	☐
14. I often eat too hurriedly.	☐	☐	☐	☐	☐	☐	☐	☐
15. I carefully observe safety rules.	☐	☐	☐	☐	☐	☐	☐	☐
16. I have some habits that are harmful to my health.	☐	☐	☐	☐	☐	☐	☐	☐
17. I become tired easily.	☐	☐	☐	☐	☐	☐	☐	☐
18. I frequently work at night or overtime.	☐	☐	☐	☐	☐	☐	☐	☐
19. I have definite goals for physical fitness.	☐	☐	☐	☐	☐	☐	☐	☐
20. I clearly understand the importance of good physical development in relation to other goals in my life.	☐	☐	☐	☐	☐	☐	☐	☐
21. I feel depressed frequently.	☐	☐	☐	☐	☐	☐	☐	☐
22. I am generally happy.	☐	☐	☐	☐	☐	☐	☐	☐
23. I experience frequent shifts in mood.	☐	☐	☐	☐	☐	☐	☐	☐

SELF-EVALUATION INVENTORY
Mental and Educational

Respond to each item below by placing an "X" in the box that best expresses the accuracy of each statement as the description of you and your habits. If the statement is not like you at all, check box number one. If it fits you perfectly, check box number seven. The boxes in between allow you to indicate varying degrees of fit.

When you have checked all items, review your ratings and indicate in the box labeled "plus or minus" whether you are satisfied with your honest rating of yourself. Enter a plus (+) if you are pleased with your rating or a minus (-) if you feel a need for a change. The "minus signs" you enter may become suggestions for concrete goal setting in this area.

1 = poor description, 7 = perfect description

	1	2	3	4	5	6	7	+ or -
1. I am an intelligent person.	☐	☐	☐	☐	☐	☐	☐	☐
2. I receive deep satisfaction from learning.	☐	☐	☐	☐	☐	☐	☐	☐
3. I have enough knowledge to do my work well.	☐	☐	☐	☐	☐	☐	☐	☐
4. I like to know about subjects not necessarily connected with my work.	☐	☐	☐	☐	☐	☐	☐	☐
5. I enjoy reading good books.	☐	☐	☐	☐	☐	☐	☐	☐
6. I have an inquiring mind.	☐	☐	☐	☐	☐	☐	☐	☐
7. I consider myself well educated.	☐	☐	☐	☐	☐	☐	☐	☐
8. I enjoy learning for learning's sake.	☐	☐	☐	☐	☐	☐	☐	☐
9. I need more education or training in some areas.	☐	☐	☐	☐	☐	☐	☐	☐
10. I could improve my income or my success in my job by gaining increased knowledge and/or skills.	☐	☐	☐	☐	☐	☐	☐	☐
11. I keep up with current trends and discoveries in my field.	☐	☐	☐	☐	☐	☐	☐	☐

	1	2	3	4	5	6	7	+ or -
12. I make active use of my imagination and creativity.	☐	☐	☐	☐	☐	☐	☐	☐
13. I have participated in some formal learning situation such as a class, seminar, extension, or correspondence course in the last three years.	☐	☐	☐	☐	☐	☐	☐	☐
14. I schedule regular time for study, research, or learning.	☐	☐	☐	☐	☐	☐	☐	☐

SELF-EVALUATION INVENTORY
Family and Home

Respond to each item below by placing an "X" in the box that best expresses the accuracy of each statement as the description of you and your habits. If the statement is not like you at all, check box number one. If it fits you perfectly, check box number seven. The boxes in between allow you to indicate varying degrees of fit.

When you have checked all items, review your ratings and indicate in the box labeled "plus or minus" whether you are satisfied with your honest rating of yourself. Enter a plus (+) if you are pleased with your rating or a minus (-) if you feel a need for a change. The "minus signs" you enter may become suggestions for concrete goal setting in this area.

1 = poor description, 7 = perfect description

	1	2	3	4	5	6	7	+ or -
1. I maintain good relationships and open communication with all members of my family.	☐	☐	☐	☐	☐	☐	☐	☐
2. I show courtesy and consideration for each member of my family.	☐	☐	☐	☐	☐	☐	☐	☐
3. I am willing to compromise when differences exist.	☐	☐	☐	☐	☐	☐	☐	☐
4. I respect the right of each family member to hold beliefs and convictions which differ from mine.	☐	☐	☐	☐	☐	☐	☐	☐

	1	2	3	4	5	6	7	+ or -
5. I make a serious effort to deal constructively with any problems that arise in my family.	☐	☐	☐	☐	☐	☐	☐	☐
6. I never make derogatory comparisons between the behavior of some member of my family and anyone else.	☐	☐	☐	☐	☐	☐	☐	☐
7. I allow the members of my family the psychological freedom to be individuals in their own right.	☐	☐	☐	☐	☐	☐	☐	☐
8. I can express disagreement with some other member of the family without unpleasant emotional scenes.	☐	☐	☐	☐	☐	☐	☐	☐
9. I can forgive and forget after a disagreement or quarrel.	☐	☐	☐	☐	☐	☐	☐	☐
10. My attitudes and behavior contribute to meeting the needs for self-esteem and self-respect of other members of my family.	☐	☐	☐	☐	☐	☐	☐	☐
11. I plan and carry through with entertainment and relaxation designed to bring family members closer together.	☐	☐	☐	☐	☐	☐	☐	☐
12. I do not feel jealous of the time that members of my family spend with outside friends.	☐	☐	☐	☐	☐	☐	☐	☐
13. I express my affection and love for each member of my family.	☐	☐	☐	☐	☐	☐	☐	☐
14. I enjoy mealtime with my family.	☐	☐	☐	☐	☐	☐	☐	☐
15. I understand clearly what other members of my family expect of me.	☐	☐	☐	☐	☐	☐	☐	☐
16. I have definite goals for making a contribution to good family relations.	☐	☐	☐	☐	☐	☐	☐	☐
17. I exercise appropriate leadership in my family.	☐	☐	☐	☐	☐	☐	☐	☐
18. I support the efforts of other family members as they work toward their goals.	☐	☐	☐	☐	☐	☐	☐	☐

SELF-EVALUATION INVENTORY
Spiritual and Ethical

Respond to each item below by placing an "X" in the box that best expresses the accuracy of each statement as the description of you and your habits. If the statement is not like you at all, check box number one. If it fits you perfectly, check box number seven. The boxes in between allow you to indicate varying degrees of fit.

When you have checked all items, review your ratings and indicate in the box labeled "plus or minus" whether you are satisfied with your honest rating of yourself. Enter a plus (+) if you are pleased with your rating or a minus (-) if you feel a need for a change. The "minus signs" you enter may become suggestions for concrete goal setting in this area.

1 = poor description, 7 = perfect description

	1	2	3	4	5	6	7	+ or -
1. I have strong religious beliefs.	☐	☐	☐	☐	☐	☐	☐	☐
2. I am basically a truthful person.	☐	☐	☐	☐	☐	☐	☐	☐
3. I consider spiritual and ethical values important in my life.	☐	☐	☐	☐	☐	☐	☐	☐
4. I love other people.	☐	☐	☐	☐	☐	☐	☐	☐
5. It is important to me to help others.	☐	☐	☐	☐	☐	☐	☐	☐
6. I tend to hold grudges rather than freely forgive.	☐	☐	☐	☐	☐	☐	☐	☐
7. I sympathize with underprivileged people.	☐	☐	☐	☐	☐	☐	☐	☐
8. I am constantly developing a better character.	☐	☐	☐	☐	☐	☐	☐	☐
9. I practice sincerely the religious beliefs I hold.	☐	☐	☐	☐	☐	☐	☐	☐
10. I am a law-abiding citizen.	☐	☐	☐	☐	☐	☐	☐	☐
11. I am a person who can be trusted.	☐	☐	☐	☐	☐	☐	☐	☐
12. I have a sense of purpose in my life.	☐	☐	☐	☐	☐	☐	☐	☐

	1	2	3	4	5	6	7	+ or -
13. My system of values places character ahead of pleasure.	☐	☐	☐	☐	☐	☐	☐	☐
14. I am judgmental of other people.	☐	☐	☐	☐	☐	☐	☐	☐
15. I frequently feel guilty.	☐	☐	☐	☐	☐	☐	☐	☐
16. I am basically selfish.	☐	☐	☐	☐	☐	☐	☐	☐
17. Freedom is more important to me than goodness.	☐	☐	☐	☐	☐	☐	☐	☐
18. I like to share with others.	☐	☐	☐	☐	☐	☐	☐	☐
19. Having high morals is important to me.	☐	☐	☐	☐	☐	☐	☐	☐
20. I try to exercise a good moral and ethical influence on others.	☐	☐	☐	☐	☐	☐	☐	☐
21. I would rather be rejected by my friends than sacrifice my principles.	☐	☐	☐	☐	☐	☐	☐	☐
22. My choices and decisions are strongly affected by my values.	☐	☐	☐	☐	☐	☐	☐	☐
23. I am an active member of a religious group which reflects my own commitments.	☐	☐	☐	☐	☐	☐	☐	☐

SELF-EVALUATION INVENTORY
Social and Cultural

Respond to each item below by placing an "X" in the box that best expresses the accuracy of each statement as the description of you and your habits. If the statement is not like you at all, check box number one. If it fits you perfectly, check box number seven. The boxes in between allow you to indicate varying degrees of fit.

When you have checked all items, review your ratings and indicate in the box labeled "plus or minus" whether you are satisfied with your honest rating of yourself. Enter a plus (+) if you are pleased with your rating or a minus (-) if you feel a need for a change. The "minus signs" you enter may become suggestions for concrete goal setting in this area.

1 = poor description, 7 = perfect description

	1	2	3	4	5	6	7	+ or -
1. I feel at ease in any social gathering.	☐	☐	☐	☐	☐	☐	☐	☐
2. I have many friends.	☐	☐	☐	☐	☐	☐	☐	☐
3. I have pleasing social manners.	☐	☐	☐	☐	☐	☐	☐	☐
4. People consider me courteous.	☐	☐	☐	☐	☐	☐	☐	☐
5. I like most people.	☐	☐	☐	☐	☐	☐	☐	☐
6. I tend to trust people too much.	☐	☐	☐	☐	☐	☐	☐	☐
7. I always strive to be the center of attention in any social situation.	☐	☐	☐	☐	☐	☐	☐	☐
8. I have many fears.	☐	☐	☐	☐	☐	☐	☐	☐
9. I am careful never to gossip about others.	☐	☐	☐	☐	☐	☐	☐	☐
10. I control my temper.	☐	☐	☐	☐	☐	☐	☐	☐
11. I have a good sense of humor.	☐	☐	☐	☐	☐	☐	☐	☐
12. I care about what others think.	☐	☐	☐	☐	☐	☐	☐	☐

	1	2	3	4	5	6	7	+ or -
13. I tend to be a leader rather than a follower.	☐	☐	☐	☐	☐	☐	☐	☐
14. Most people like me.	☐	☐	☐	☐	☐	☐	☐	☐
15. I am a self-confident person.	☐	☐	☐	☐	☐	☐	☐	☐
16. I can follow as well as lead.	☐	☐	☐	☐	☐	☐	☐	☐
17. I can get along with people of different types.	☐	☐	☐	☐	☐	☐	☐	☐
18. I respect the right of others to hold opinions different from mine.	☐	☐	☐	☐	☐	☐	☐	☐
19. I can discuss controversial subjects without becoming upset.	☐	☐	☐	☐	☐	☐	☐	☐
20. I feel a responsibility for helping my community improve.	☐	☐	☐	☐	☐	☐	☐	☐

ANALYSIS

Now write a list of 20 things you enjoy doing and goals you would like to achieve. These may include hobbies, amusement, social activities, sports, classes etc. Next, read the following list of questions and thoughts. Think about each. Write your answers to the questions on a separate piece of paper to use as a guide later.

How would your life change if you learned you only had six months to live? How would you spend your time? Where would you go? What would you do? Would you choose to notice flowers, trees and nature more? Of what do you think you might take more notice? The problem is that most of the time we do not take the time to enjoy the here and now. We are always looking to the future or the past.

Most of us drift along in a dream state, especially if we are doing something monotonous like driving a long distance. We sort of move into a trance. If you are sitting down, close your eyes for a moment and feel and hear the sensations around you. What do you hear? What do you feel on your body? See, you were in the present if only for one moment.

In what ways would your life change if you were to win one million dollars cash, tax free, tomorrow? Visualize yourself spending or using the money. Would you give some to your family? Would you buy a new house or a new car or retire? Most people think they will never have millions of dollars, but with proper goal setting, planning and time, most goals are achievable.

What could you accomplish if there was no fear in the way? I remember when I started my financial planning business I was afraid to charge people to prepare the financial plan for them. It wasn't done in those days. You made money by selling a product like insurance. With great trepidation because I didn't want to lose clients, I began charging $300 per client. I was amazed. Not only were they willing to pay the fee, but they bought more products. No matter what your dreams are, if you never attempt to achieve them they will never come to fruition.

What activities have brought you the greatest amount of joy and fulfillment? What is your passion? Do you have a hobby? My passion is goal setting. I know that if people set goals they will get further in life. I put my passion and my work together, so that I now work at what I love.

How much money would it take to allow you to live a comfortable lifestyle that would afford you the ability to do the activities you enjoy while bringing you fulfillment and well being? It is a tough question. You must be realistic about it. Think of what you would like to be earning a year from now. How about three years? Five years? If you make these figures one of your goals and use proper goal setting techniques, you should be able to achieve the desired results.

And then there's retirement. With proper goal setting you can retire with the net worth that you desire when you have completed your working years. This is the nest egg for your retirement. You should think about how much this amount can safely generate for you per month, leaving a comfortable buffer. Of course you have to take inflation into account when arriving at this number.

You can't know what you don't know until you know it. If you do not know what it is like to make the amount of money that you want to be earning, look around you at those who do, people who are in the financial situation in which you would like to be. This will help you determine how to make the kind of money you would like to make. It should also give you ideas about how to increase your sales, if that is your line of work.

Ask yourself, as you view another, 'What is he/she is doing differently from me which enables him/her to earn that kind of money?' Most people enjoy being asked what they are doing to achieve success. If you ask them, listen to what they say. More than likely you will find ways to increase your own business.

Now let's talk about creating life area goals. The following are items helpful to consider when putting together your list of goals.

When creating career and professional goals it is important to consider what your strengths are, what comes easily to you, and at what you are good. There is a book out called *Do What You Love-The Money Will Follow.* That is true. You will be much happier at your job if you do what you love. You can always obtain training in the profession of your choice to enable you to start working in that profession.

With physical and health goals it is important to take into account the way you feel during the day. Do you feel that you have enough energy and stamina and are you comfortable with the appearance of your body? If you find a way to work out that you enjoy, working out will become a lot easier for you. It can even be fun. I like to ride a bicycle. I try to do so at least five days a week for a half-hour. I also try to go to the gym three times a week. This is a chore for me, because I don't like working out with weights. I do so because it is good for me mentally and physically. When my schedule makes it necessary to skip one of these workout methods, guess which one I wind up skipping!

Personal development goals consist of any area in which you would like to expand your knowledge. Going to night school, learning a new language, and learning to play a musical instrument are all such endeavors.

When considering family and relationship goals, take a look at your family life as it is right now. Are you as close to your family as you would like to be? Would you like to be closer? Is there a problem between you and your siblings? How are things going with you and your children? Can you think of things that you can do to enhance and improve these relationships? Sometimes you have a little crow eating at you about peace and harmony. You need to ask yourself, 'Am I willing to do what it takes to make peace and harmony a part of my life?'

Do you have a great desire to go somewhere? A special trip you want to experience? This would be a travel goal. I have a relative whose family was in Germany. He always talked about going over there some day. That was supposedly his big dream. He had money to do so, but he never did. He died of cancer at an early age. Set your goals and don't wait to take action.

Setting material and tangible goals is easy. We all want new things like a new car, a new house, or even maybe something small and personal. A young lady who worked at my office wanted a special pair of shoes. She listed that desire as one of her goals. Later, she happily modeled her new shoes for everyone in the office. It doesn't matter what you want, put it down in writing and go for it.

When you set your community and service goals remember they need not be solely monetary. You could volunteer your time for a good cause. Choose one that you feel strongly about or you won't work as hard at it and it won't be fun. Years ago I volunteered to work at the Crystal Cathedral in Garden Grove. As I mentioned, I worked on a suicide hotline which was open 24 hours a day. While I hope and believe that I helped people, I know for sure that they helped me!

Are you creative? Do you have a skill or talent area in which you would like to work? List these as creative goals. This does not have to be something you are good at, just something that you would like to do.

Spiritual and inner development goals can include meditation, yoga, and/or attending church services. These are incredibly personal choices. What would you like to do? Choose that or those which will aid in stress reduction and personal harmony.

What intellectual and educational goals would you like to achieve? It is a proven fact that the higher one's education, the more money he makes. Is this something that you aspire to do? If so, how does education fit in to your goals or is education your goal? Will you only take classes to further your career or will you take courses at college or trade school simply to gain more knowledge about that particular topic of interest?

What one great thing would you dare to dream if you knew you could not fail? What if you were guaranteed success? You must choose to think that you can't fail. That's why I like persistence. You just keep on keeping on until you win. People who answer this question generally select something they really like to do.

Based on these exercises, what do you think should be your most important goal? What is your major definite purpose? Give some real thought to this question and write your answer in detail. This is where your major drive should be. The more detail you state, the clearer you goal will become.

TESTING YOUR MAJOR GOAL

Desire

Do you really want your goal personally, or is this something that someone else wants for you? While spouse, parents, family and friends are important in your life, your major goal is for you and no one else.

Believe

Is your goal believable and achievable? What this question means is that the goal must be believable to you, because that is what counts. If you truly believe that you have the ability to achieve your goal, it is more likely that you can and will. Naturally, it must be a goal that is physically achievable. For example, you cannot fly without any equipment no matter how hard you try or how much you would like to believe that you could.

Is it measurable? This is a biggie. Once you write it, you have committed yourself to the plan. You have begun the journey towards goal achievement. You have made a commitment to yourself. If your goal is losing weight, keep a log of the pounds lost. If it is quitting smoking, keep a log of your reduction of cigarette consumption. If the goal is tracking finances, keep track of increase in savings and reduction of debt.

Analyze

Where are you starting from now? Where are you today? Where are your assets now? (Financial, physical, mental etc.) You must take stock of and set up a base to see what you need to do to reach your goal.

Determine

How will you personally benefit from achieving your goal? List in writing the personal benefits of achieving your set goals. This will help you visualize the completion of those goals.

Time

Set a deadline for your goal. When? Commit to that time frame. This is holding your feet to the fire. I know that in my case, setting a date makes me get to work immediately. This helps me to complete whatever goals I set.

Ask

What obstacles must you overcome? You should pre-list your obstacles. Then determine how you will overcome or go around each one. You may have to enlist outside help or even go around them instead of through them.

Research

What additional information will you require? You should research and study everything possible about your goal. The more information you have about your goal, the easier it will be for you to achieve that goal. When I first became interested in hypnosis I read every book I could find on the subject. I talked to anyone who had an interest in or was knowledgeable about the subject.

Find Key People

Whose assistance or cooperation do you need to achieve your goal? Who are the key people? Take caution to select the right people. Some of your friends or your relatives may subconsciously or consciously sabotage your goal. They may feel justified in being negative toward your goal for many reasons including criticism and negativity. Choose your team carefully.

Now that you have taken the previous questions into consideration, go back and review the original list of 20 activities you enjoy doing and goals you would like to achieve. Organize them as 1=Very important 2=Important 3=Nice but not important. Finally, write a detailed plan for each of the goals that you have determined to be of prime importance. Write them out clearly. Think about what you are going to do starting today and every day until you have reached your goal. Remember, the more detailed your descriptions, the more likely you are to achieve your goals!

CHAPTER 4

GOAL SETTING DEFINED

If it is to be it is up to me.

When you have clearly defined goals from each aspect of your life you can unlock the incredible reserves that lie within you. The greatest single enemy of your potential for greater success and achievement is your comfort zone, your tendency to get stuck in a rut and then resist all change, even positive change, that would force you out. People naturally fear and avoid change. All growth, all progress, and all advancement require change. Change is inevitable. In spite of anything you do, life never goes on the same way for very long.

The first benefit of goal setting is that it allows you to control the direction of your life, ensuring that change is predominately positive and self-determined. With clear goals backed by detailed plans of action, you ensure that the changes taking place represent improvements in your life and you eliminate a major cause of fear and insecurity.

The primary requirement for success in life is the ability to set and achieve short term, medium-term and long- term goals. You either work to achieve your goals or you work to achieve someone else's goals. With goals as your dominant thoughts, you begin to attract into your life people and circumstances in harmony with those goals. You attract ideas, opportunities, and resources which can help you.

Substitute positive thoughts for negatives. Whenever something goes wrong, think about your goals. When you have a bad day, think about your goals. You likely have been told for years that you must have goals. You have been told that you have to be working toward your goals regularly. The sad fact is that very few people have any real goals at all. Less than 3 percent of men and women place goals in writing. Less than 1 percent read and review goals regularly.

SEVEN REASONS PEOPLE DO NOT SET GOALS

1. They are not serious. They want to be more successful, they want to improve their lives, but they are not willing to make the necessary effort.

2. They have not accepted responsibility for their lives. People are fully responsible for their lives and for everything that happens to them. Recognition and acceptance of those are prerequisites for goal setting.

3. They harbor deep-seated feelings of guilt and unworthiness. Until they forgive and/or value themselves, they will not move forward.

4. They do not realize the importance of goals. If people realized how important goals are to a happy, successful life, far more people would have goals than do.

5. They don't know how. You can earn a university degree, the equivalent of fifteen or sixteen years of education, and never receive an hour's worth of instruction on goal setting, though goal setting may be more important to your long term happiness than any other single subject.

6. They fear rejection or criticism. Siblings and friends may laugh at us and ridicule us for thinking about being someone or doing something beyond what they imagine for themselves. The solution to fear of criticism or sounding foolish is simple: Keep your goals confidential. Don't tell anybody. All effective goal-setters finally learn to keep their goals to themselves. There are two exceptions to this practice of confidentiality. The first are the people (such as boss or spouse) whose help you will need to achieve your goals. Second, are other goal-oriented people who will encourage you in the direction you want to go.

7. Most predominantly, people do not set goals due to fear of failure. Fear of failure is the greatest single obstacle to success in adult life. Ironically, it is impossible to succeed without failing. After Edison had conducted more than 5,000 experiments a young journalist came to him and asked him why he persisted after having failed more than 5,000 times. Edison is said to have replied, "Young man, you don't understand how the world works. I have not failed at all. I have successfully identified 5,000 ways that it will not work. That just puts me 5,000 ways closer to the way that will."

Napoleon Hill said, "Seek within each setback the valuable lesson that it contains."

Keep looking for the good. Lessons learned from setbacks make ultimate success possible. You can learn to overcome fear of failure by being absolutely clear about your goals and by accepting that temporary setbacks and obstacles are the inevitable price one pays to achieve any great success in life.

THE FIVE PRINCIPLES OF GOAL SETTING

1. Congruency

Your goals and your values must fit together like a hand in a glove.

2. Area of Excellence

Each person has the capacity to be excellent at something and perhaps several things. Your area of excellence is invariably doing what you most enjoy and doing it well.

3. Acres of Diamonds Concept

Your acres of diamonds probably lie in your own talents, your interests, your education, your background and experience, your industry, your city, your contacts.

4. Balance

You need a variety of goals in the eight critical areas of life in order to perform at your best.

- Financial and Career
- Social and Cultural
- Emotional
- Friends and Family
- Mental and Intellectual

- Health
- Spiritual and Ethical
- Physical

To maintain proper balance you need two or three goals in each area, a total of twelve to eighteen goals in all.

5. Determination of Major Life-Purpose

Your major purpose is your number-one goal, the goal that is more important to you than the accomplishment of any other single goal or objective at this time. The way you choose your overarching goal is by analyzing all your goals and asking, "Which goal, if I accomplish it, would do the most to help me achieve all my other goals?"

GOAL SETTING RULES

Your goals must be in harmony with one another, not contradictory. You cannot have a goal to be financially successful or to build your own successful business and simultaneously have a goal to spend half your day at the golf course or beach.

Your goals must be challenging. When you initially set goals, they should have about a 50 percent or better probability of success. This level of probability is ideal for motivation, yet not so difficult that you become easily discouraged.

You should have both tangible and intangible goals, both quantitative and qualitative. You should have concrete goals that you can measure and evaluate objectively. At the same time, you should have qualitative goals, for your inner life and your relationships.

Additionally, you need short term, medium-term, and

long-term goals. You need goals for today and goals for five, ten and twenty years from today. The ideal short-term goal for business, career, and personal planning is about ninety days. The ideal longer-term period for the same goals is two to three years. The best major purpose goal is aimed at two or three years out. You can then break it down into ninety-day segments, and subsequently break those down to monthly, weekly and daily subgoals with measurable benchmarks to enable you to assess your progress. The decision to become a goal-setting, goal-achieving, future-focused person gives you tremendous sense of self-control. Your self-esteem increases as you progress towards your goals. You like and respect yourself more and more. Your personality improves and you become a more positive, confident person. You feel happy and excited about life.

HOW TO IDENTIFY YOUR GOALS

Here are seven goal-setting questions for you to ask and answer over and over again.

1. What are your five most important values in life?

What is really important to you? Once you have identified the five most important things in life, organize them in order of priority, from number one, most important, through number five. Choosing and defining your values and their order of importance comes before setting your goals.

2. What are your three most important goals in life right now?

Write the answer to this question within thirty seconds.

This is called the "quick list" method. Your top three will just pop into your conscious mind.

3. What would you do, how would you spend your time, if you learned today that you only had six months to live?

4. What would you do if you won a million dollars cash, tax free, in the lottery tomorrow?

How would you change your life? What would you buy? What would you start or stop doing? Imagine that you only have two minutes to write your answers and you will only be able to acquire what you have written.

5. What have you always wanted to do but have been afraid to attempt?

6. What do you most enjoy? What gives you the most self-esteem and personal satisfaction?

The most successful men and women in America are invariably doing what they really enjoy.

7. What one great thing would you dare to dream if you knew you could not fail?

What one exciting goal would you set for yourself?

The very fact that you could write whatever you wrote in answer to any of these questions means that you can achieve it. The only question you have to answer is, "Do I want it badly enough and am I willing to pay the price?" Take a few minutes and write out your answers to each of these seven questions. Once you have your answers on paper, go over them and select just one as your major definite purpose in life right now. By the simple act of deciding what you really want and writing it down, you will have moved yourself into the top 3 percent. You will have done something that few people ever do. You will have established a written set of goals for yourself. You are now ready to make a giant leap forward.

Develop a habit of continuous goal setting.

To maximize your goal-achieving ability, you need a method. You need a proven process that you can use over and over, with any goal, in any situation, to bring all the powers of your mind to bear on accomplishing whatever it is you desire.

THE TWELVE-STEP SYSTEM

The twelve-step system is perhaps the most effective goal-achieving process ever developed. It has been used by hundreds of thousands of men and women all over the world to revolutionize their lives. Corporations use it to reorganize and go on to greater sales and profitability. It is simple (as all true things are) but it is so astonishingly effective that it continues to amaze even the most skeptical people.

Step One: Develop desire-intense, burning desire.

If you dwell upon your desires, if you think about them and write them out and make plans to accomplish them continually, your desires eventually become so strong that they override and push aside your fears. Intense, burning desire for a specific goal enables you to rise above your fears and move forward over any obstacles. Desire is personal.

Step Two: Develop belief.

You must absolutely believe that it is possible for you to achieve your goal. Belief is the catalyst that activates you mental powers, so it is important that your goals be realistic, especially at first. If your goal is to earn more money, you should set a goal to increase your income by 10, 20, or 30 percent over the next twelve months. These are believable goals. If your goal is too far beyond anything you've accomplished in the past, setting it too high actually makes it a de-motivator. You become discouraged more easily and you can soon stop believing that it is possible for you. If you want to lose weight, set a goal to lose five pounds over the next thirty to sixty days, as well as a long-term goal of thirty to fifty pounds over a longer period of time. Concentrate on the short-term goal. Use the longer-term goal as a guideline.

Step Three: Place your goals in writing.

Goals that are not in writing are not goals at all. They are merely wishes or fantasies. A wish is a goal with no energy behind it. One of the most powerful of all methods for implanting a goal into your subconscious mind is to write it out clearly, vividly, in detail, exactly as you would like to see it in reality. Don't worry for the moment about how the goal is going to be achieved. Your main job in the beginning is to be absolutely certain about exactly what it is that you desire, not to worry about the process of achieving it.

Step Four: Make a list of all the ways that you will benefit from achieving your goal.

Keep your desire burning brightly by continually thinking of all the benefits, satisfactions and rewards you will enjoy as a result of achieving your goal. Make a list of all benefits, tangible and intangible, that you can possibly enjoy as a result of achieving your goal. The longer the list, the more motivated and determined you will become.

Step Five: Analyze your starting position.

If you decide to lose weight, the very first thing you need to do is to weigh yourself. If you want to achieve a certain net worth, the first thing you should do is create a personal financial statement to find out how much you are worth today.

Step Six: Set a deadline.

Set deadlines on all tangible, measurable goals. Don't set deadlines on intangible goals. What if you set a goal and a deadline and you don't achieve it by your deadline? Simple: You set another deadline. It just means that you're not ready yet. You guessed wrong. You were too optimistic. If you don't achieve your goal by your new deadline, you set still another deadline until you finally do achieve it. In 80 percent of cases, if goals are sufficiently realistic, plans are sufficiently detailed, and you work your plans faithfully, you will achieve your goal by your deadline. If your major definite purpose has a two, three, or five-year deadline, your next step is to break your goal down into ninety-day sub-goals. Then break the ninety-day goals down into thirty-day goals.

Start from a visualization of your goal as already accomplished and work back to the present. Imagine the steps that you would have taken to get from where you are now to where you want to be in the future. "Project forward, look backward" is a powerful technique that enables you to see possibilities and pitfalls that you might otherwise miss.

Step Seven: Make a list of all the obstacles that stand between you and the accomplishment of your goal.

What is the single biggest obstacle that stands between you and your goal? Almost invariably, there is one big rock or major obstacle that lies across your path and blocks your progress.

Step Eight: Identify the additional information you will need to achieve your goal.

Can you hire someone else with this knowledge? Can you employ someone temporarily, such as a consultant, or a specialist, with the knowledge you require? Who else has achieved success in your particular field, and could you go to him or her for advice? Make a list of all the information, talents, skills, abilities and experience you will need and then make a plan to learn, buy, rent or borrow this information or skill as quickly as possible.

Step Nine: Make a list of all the people whose help and cooperation you will require.

Take this list and organize it in order of priority. Whose help is the most important? Whose help is the second most important?

Other people will help you achieve your goals only if they feel that they will be compensated for their efforts in some way. No one works for nothing. Everyone has his or her own personal motivation. Ask yourself the question, 'What am I going to do for them to get them to help me?'

Successful people and successful businesses are those which always exceed expectations, who always do more than is expected of them. Find and be this type of person!

Step Ten: Make a plan.

Write in detail what you want, when you want it, why you want it and where you are starting. Make a list of the obstacles you must overcome, the information you will require, and the people whose help you will need. In other words, compile the information acquired as you walked through steps 1 through 9.

A plan organized by priority lists activities in their order of importance. What is the most important thing that you have to do? The second most important thing? Accept feedback and make course corrections along the way.

Step Eleven: Use visualization.

Create a clear mental picture of your goal as it would appear if it were already achieved. Each time you visualize your goal as accomplished, you increase your desire and intensify your belief that the goal is achievable to you. What you see is what you get.

You immediately begin attracting to you, like iron filings to a magnet, the people, ideas, and opportunities you need to attain you objectives.

Step Twelve: Make the decision, in advance, that you will never give up.

The longer you persist, the more convinced and determined you become. You finally reach the point where nothing can stop you. And nothing will.

DON'T QUIT

When things go wrong, as they sometimes will,
When the road you're trudging seems all uphill,
When the funds are low and the debts are high,
And you want to smile but you have to sigh,
When care is pressing you down a bit
Rest if you must, but don't you quit.
For life is queer with its twists and turns,
As every one of us sometimes learns,
And many a failure turns about,
When he might have won if he'd stuck it out.
Success is just failure turned inside out,
The silver tint of the clouds of doubt.
And you never can tell how close you are,
It may be near when it seems so far.
So stick to the fight when you're hardest hit,
It's when things seem worst that *you must not quit!*

– *Anonymous*

It takes a large amount of energy to get a body from a resting position to a state of forward motion; it takes a smaller amount of energy to keep it in motion at the same speed. This is one of the most important of all principles underlying great success. Develop a success habit by doing something every single day to move you toward your goals. Review goals every morning and think about them throughout every day. Always look for something you can do to contribute to their achievement.

CHAPTER 5

CREATING YOUR LIFE PLAN

Happiness is found in doing, not merely possessing.

We have thus far plotted points, or goals, on the map of your life journey. Now we will talk about the road to get there, your life plan. The following pages contain gauges which will help you monitor and manage your journey. The first gauge for you to fill out is the Goal Circle. The goal circle is like the speedometer on your car. Look at each of your goals for each goal category. How fast do you want to get there? How much "fuel" do you want to use for each goal? What sacrifices in other areas are you willing to make?

Using a pen of one color, plot where you feel you are currently on the Goal Circle for each section. Total dissatisfaction with a particular portion of your life would be marked near the 0% at the circle's center. Conversely, complete satisfaction would be indicated by creating a line at the circle's outer edge (100%). When you have completed that, use a pen of a different color to plot where you would like to be within each section of the circle.

See example:

100%

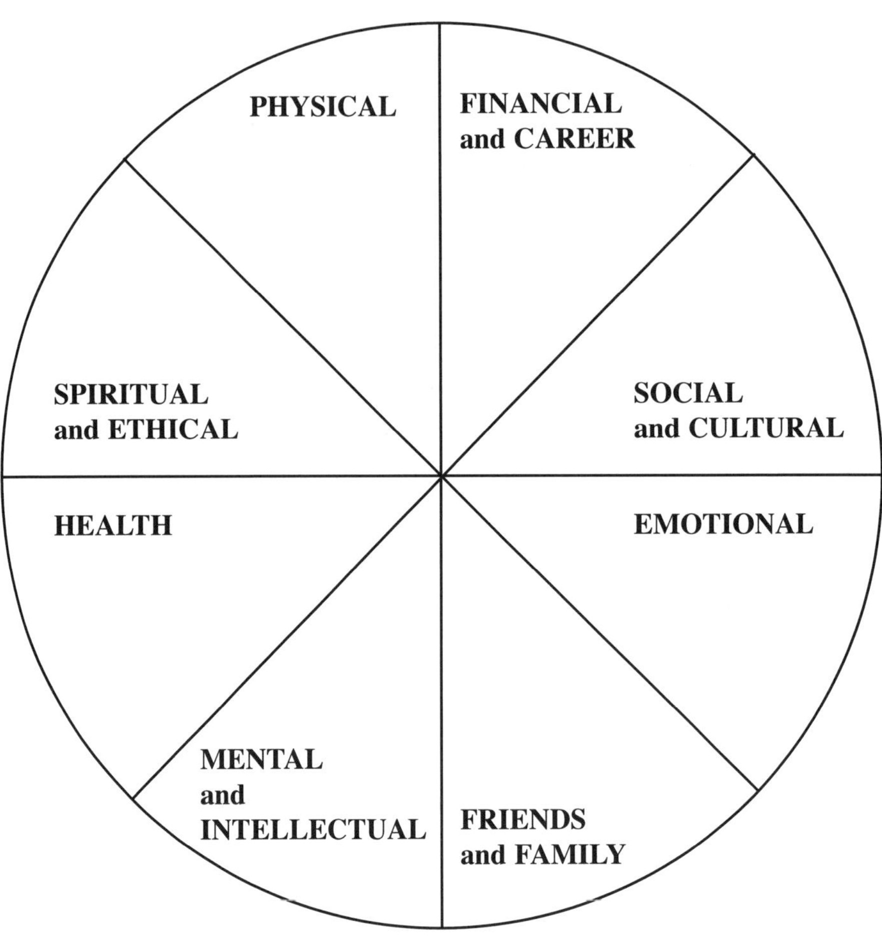
PHYSICAL
FINANCIAL and CAREER
SPIRITUAL and ETHICAL
SOCIAL and CULTURAL
HEALTH
EMOTIONAL
MENTAL and INTELLECTUAL
FRIENDS and FAMILY

Your Life Plan

By creating your life plan you identify the mile markers that you must pass on your journey to fulfill your goals.

Resolve to fill out your action plan using one page every day. Begin with today's date and immediately write down your five most important goals. Write out your definite purpose in the present tense as if it were already a reality. For example,

1. I am acquiring 5 new accounts today.

a. I will call 20 leads today.

b. I will arrange a lunch meeting with Mr. Johnson today.

c. I will call everyone on my follow-up list.

2. I am taking 15 minutes to meditate and pray today.

a. I will close the door and turn off the television and phone for 15 minutes.

b. I will go to a private place, close my eyes, inhale, hold for 7 seconds. Exhale, relax.

3. I am taking time to play a game with my family tonight.

a. I will have all my work completed and filed by 4:45 so that I can leave the office on time.

b. I will call ahead to make sure the kids have their home work finished by the time I get home.

c. I will bring home takeout so that there will be no cook ing or clean-up tonight.

4. I am improving my lap time today by two seconds from yesterday's time.

a. I will make sure to have a good stretch before my workout.

b. I will breathe more effectively.

c. I will visualize proper technique and success.

5. I am reading a chapter of ***Think and Grow Rich*** *or some other positive self-help book today.*

a. After the kids go to bed I will go in the study and read until the chapter is completed.

b. I will write down and act on one idea from that chapter.

Write your major problem or goal for the day at the top of the page in the form of a question.

Example:
What can I do today to assure that I will meet quota for May in order to make commission?

Write out twenty possible solutions for this question.

Next, select your action commitments for today from the list of twenty solutions that you just created and write them at the bottom of the page.

1. I will follow up with clients who haven't made a recent order.
2. I will call 5 leads today.
3. I will go to local networking meeting to obtain new clients.
4. I will suggest add-on items to current clients calling in orders.
5. I will email information to all clients on my list about our newest product.

Begin immediately to take action! Get going. Work steadily toward the achievement of your goals throughout the day. It takes about thirty-one days to form a habit, so repeat this process every single day for at least thirty-one days until it becomes your habit.

Now that you have an idea about the daily process, select your five most important life goals and write out ten activities for each that you could start doing immediately to turn them into realities. Organize your ten action steps in order of importance. Repeat this procedure for all five of your goals.

GOAL NUMBER _______:

____

ACTION STEPS ORDER

1. ________________________________ __________

2. ________________________________ __________

3. ________________________________ __________

4. ________________________________ __________

5. ________________________________ __________

6. ________________________________ __________

7. ________________________________ __________

8. ________________________________ __________

9. ________________________________ __________

10. ________________________________ __________

Organize your action steps in the right-hand column in order of importance to achieving your goal, from #1 to #10.

ACTION PLAN: ______________________________

____

____

____

____

____

In order to form goal-setting habits, set up a thirty-one day calendar. On the page following I have inserted a sample of day number one, with the directions to help you achieve your top five goals. Create and use a daily worksheet for one entire month. At the end of that month begin a Day One for the start of the following month. Proceed in that manner until your goal is fully achieved!

DAY __________

____

DATE BACKGROUND IDEA FOR TODAY

Daily Goal Planning Exercise- Quick List My five most important goals are:

- ____
- ____
- ____
- ____
- ____

Daily Goal Setting Exercise- My major definite purpose is:

____

____

____

____

Daily Goal Planning Exercise- My plans (written in longhand using the present tense) are:

____

____

____

____

____

My major problem or goal (in the form of a question) is:

____

____

____

____

____

20 answers to the preceding question are:

1. ______________________________
2. ______________________________
3. ______________________________
4. ______________________________
5. ______________________________
6. ______________________________
7. ______________________________
8. ______________________________
9. ______________________________
10. ______________________________
11. ______________________________
12. ______________________________
13. ______________________________
14. ______________________________
15. ______________________________
16. ______________________________
17. ______________________________
18. ______________________________
19. ______________________________
20. ______________________________

One action from the preceding exercise to begin immediately is:

____

____

____

____

The following page contains a self-actualization table. This table is designed for you to fill out each day during the week for a month in order for you to be conscious of the decision-making changes that your are undertaking.

You will note the lines for different activities which, when managed properly, can help you get to your goals and live a healthier lifestyle.

Up at (Time)

Make a habit of rising the same time each day. If depression is a challenge for you, you will make a conscious effort to get up and get active, which will help reduce depression.

Positive Affirmation

Choose a positive affirmation(s) appropriate for what is happening in your life that you can believe and state several times daily to assist you in working through that portion of your life.

Exercise

Exercise in some manner each day for good health and stress reduction.

Drink Water

Drink water to hydrate and cleanse the body.

Positive Reading

Do this daily, even if only for a couple of minutes. This reduces depression and dispels negativity, putting you in a positive state of mind for positive results.

Goal Sheets

Fill out the goal sheets to assist in forming conscious decision-making changes. These will measure your success and progress toward your goals.

Visualization

One of your strongest senses in helping you to achieve your goals, the time you spend visualizing your goals empowers your mind, making success more likely to occur.

Stop Food at (Time)

In order to manage your weight and to enjoy a good night's rest it is important to stop the intake of food two hours before going to bed. If you go to bed at 10 p.m. it is recommended that you stop food intake at 8 p.m.

Hypnosis Tape

Take time to listen to the tape for thirty-one consecutive days to help positive habit development.

In Bed By (Time)

Form a positive rest cycle that your body will become accustomed to. This will make it easier to fall asleep at night.

DATE	Sunday	Monday	Tuesday	Wednesday	Thursday	Friday	Saturday
UP AT (TIME)							
POSITIVE AFFIRMATION							
EXERCISE							
DRINK							
WATER							
POSITIVE READING							
GOAL SHEETS							
VISUALIZATION							
STOP FOOD AT (TIME)							
SELF-HYPNOSIS TAPE							
IN BED BY (TIME)							

SECTION THREE: Resources and Tools for Goal Setting

CHAPTER 6

MASTER MIND ALLIANCE

How To Create A Master Mind Alliance

The benefit of involving others in your goals and plans is instant access to experience, knowledge, and wisdom. There will come a time when uncertainty will arrive. That's why having another set of eyes and ears is essential. That is the purpose of a Master Mind Alliance.

The Purpose of a Master Mind Alliance

According to Napoleon Hill, "A Master Mind Alliance is the coordination of knowledge and effort, in a spirit of harmony, between two or more people, for the attainment of a definite purpose."

A Master Mind Alliance stimulates dialog among thinking people, encouraging them to share their ideas and experiences, successes and failures, as a means of fostering individual and collective achievement. A Master Mind Alliance is the balanced focusing of minds and attentions on a specific goal that multiplies effectiveness and produces greater results in a shorter period of time.

Why Start a Master Mind Alliance?

In today's turbulent world, we are confronted with many unknowns. Surviving and prospering means keeping up with new ideas. Joining others in a Master Mind Alliance-either with people within your organization, industry, or some other interest group provides impetus for keeping up with change and positions us for rapidly opening and closing opportunities.

What Are the Benefits of a Master Mind Alliance?

An effective Master Mind Alliance is a conduit for:

- A trusting environment in which a confidential exchange of ideas can flourish.
- Creative problem-solving on both professional and personal issues.
- Skill development and personal growth.
- Advice, collective support, and accountability to oneself and others.
- Leveraging the intelligence and real-world experience of others.
- Achieving far more than one could ever achieve on one's own due to the insights and wisdom of others.

How Do You Find Interested Participants?

Be patient when building your Master Mind Alliance. The most important thing is the chemistry. Put the same thought and energy into choosing participants as you would into any major life decision. Participants can be found in any number of places:

Within your Organization – You may ask colleagues within your department or from other departments throughout the company to participate in the group.

Outside your Organization- Ask competitors, suppliers, people in similar industries, or associates from totally different industries to get involved.

In Your Community- Ask family, friends, neighbors, members of professional associations to which you belong, members of your church or synagogue, or members of other types of groups to participate.

Begin with trust and make a list of people you know who are headed in the same direction as you, people with similar values and ambitions. Keep in mind that your goal is not to create a mentor-protégé relationship, but a peer-to-peer relationship.

It is recommended that Master Mind Alliance members bring varied professional backgrounds. This diversity can and will provide a wide base of knowledge and experience just as a Board of Directors does for a corporation.

How Often Should You Meet?

For most Master Mind alliances, meeting once per week or every two weeks is optimal. If you meet less frequently, the group never gets any momentum going and synergy is lost. If your group's purpose is professional or organizational development, you may find people are motivated to meet more often. It is a good idea to meet on some predictable day, such as the first and third Wednesday of every month.

Where Should You Meet?

If this is a Master Mind within one organization, you could choose a conference room within the company's offices. If it is a professional or personal group not connected to any one organization, you could rotate among members' homes or use library rooms, local community centers, coffee shops, large bookstores, churches, etc.

Consistency is important to creating an effective Master Mind Alliance. Meeting in the same place and at the same time is an excellent idea. This will allow each member to best protect the goals of the group from other clamoring commitments.

Consider having water, juice, coffee, or tea available as the smallest things can be useful in producing favorable mood and environment. Be sure that distractions are kept to a minimum: no phones, no pagers, and no disturbances from other rooms or people.

Email discussion is a useful tool for Master Mind groups for the following reasons:

- Convenience
- Can be viewed and responded to at any time during the day.
- More complete
- Meeting topics can be discussed for days or weeks and by a greater number of participants.
- No constraints as far as meeting time or space.

What is the Facilitator's Job?

The facilitator may be the same person each time or members may choose a rotation system, depending on the needs and wants of the group.

The facilitator:

- Monitors start and stop times while maintaining order and purpose.
- Leads the group through its agenda in a timely manner.
- Senses the pulse of the group and monitors its progress.
- Exemplifies a spirit of openness.
- Delivers appropriate feedback where necessary.
- Encourages dialog from all participants, especially those who are stuck, quiet or shy.
- Reviews the topic carefully for specific discussion questions.

Start-Up Questions

What is the First Meeting Agenda?
Where will we meet?
When will we meet?
How will we notify people of meeting locations, times, and agendas?
What are the costs involved and how will we divide them?
How will we choose topics to discuss and goals upon which to concentrate?
What are our basic ground rules?
Will we have a single facilitator or will the role rotate among the Master Mind members?

1. **Consider choosing a name for your group.**
   This provides another drop of glue that keeps the group involved, focused and having fun. Possibilities include: The Dynamic Duo, The Triple Threat, The Fabulous Four, and the High Five.

2. **Clarify your group's purpose.**
   What is the purpose of the group? Is it about ongoing mutual benefit and growing relationships? Is the group's purpose stated clearly from the outset? Groups work better when they state clear overall purpose.

3. **Be selective.**
   Don't work with just anybody. Think about your growth strategically and about who might aid you in getting where you want to be. Choose nurturing people to join you in this project. Look for naturally existing relationships (family, clients, colleagues).

4. **Obtain and maintain buy-in.**
   When attempting to achieve a goal which involves others, be sure that everyone is singing from the same sheet of music. This does not mean stamping out individual initiative, but it does mean agreeing upon common goals and the achievement of them despite any personal disharmonies or disagreements.

5. **Mix diverse talents and perspectives.**
   How well do people line up in complementary fields of experience and expertise? Bringing together people with different backgrounds and outlooks strengthens a Master

Mind Alliance.

Everyone involved in achieving the goal should have a part in establishing it. Participation in the goal-setting process helps ensure that the goal will be successfully accomplished because people have bought into its importance and method of achievement initially.

Successful buy-in requires a three-step analysis:

1. Discussion – Discuss the who, what, where, how, and why of the desired goal.
2. Compromise – Encourage give-and-take between parties. The compromise and negotiation of the goal are part of the achievement process.
3. Agreement – Seek early concurrence regarding the goal, achievement process, and assigned responsibilities.

Discussion, compromise, and agreement require that all parties interact with one another during the goal-setting process. The interaction means that people must talk! The most essential element in the early stages of developing a Master Mind Alliance is communication.

6. Have Fun!

The road to success is often bumpy and constantly under construction, but that doesn't mean you can't enjoy the ride. You will and should experience moments of deep satisfaction and fun. This is the best indicator to let you know that your Master Mind Alliance is working.

Ronald G. Miller

CHAPTER 7

SELF-HYPNOSIS TAPE SCRIPTS

I have added a chapter including self-hypnotic scripts because they will help you achieve your goals. I have included several different scripts that you can tape into your tape recorder to listen to in the morning or whenever is regularly the best time for you. Each is about thirty minutes long. You should listen to one per day. Do not listen while driving, but find a nice, quiet place where you will be able to be alone and comfortable. I find that early in the morning or just before I go to sleep at night is the best time for me. Find a routine that works well for you.

In these scripts some words are listed for direction only and are not to be stated aloud. These will be set apart by brackets. One such is **'Pause'**. Each time you see this word, simply count silently **'1-2-3'**.

Before you begin a taped session, turn off all distractions including cell phone and TV. Lie or sit down, making yourself comfortable. Wear loose clothing. Fix your eyes on a spot above the level of your eyes, so your gaze rests slightly upward.

Provide at least twenty seconds of silence at the beginning of your tape so that there is enough time to get into a comfortable position and to prepare yourself for the session.

Goal Setting Hypnosis Tape

Give good lead time (20 seconds).

I am becoming more and more relaxed.
I am concentrating on the words being said,
I am listening only to my voice.
My eyelids are getting heavier and heavier, heavier and heavier.
[Pause]
I feel like lead weights are being put on my eyelids and pulling them down, down, down.
[Pause]
Heavier, and heavier, and heavier.
My eyelids are so heavy they are starting to close.
I cannot keep them open.
I may close my eyes any time I want to.
They are getting heavier and heavier and heavier. My eyelids are closing, closing, closing. I close my eyes now, if I have not already done so. My eyelids are sealed
tight, tight, tight, together.
I am visualizing my eyelids being sealed together, just as if they were glued or zipped closed.
[Pause]
I cannot open my eyes. The harder I try, the tighter my eyes become sealed together.
[Pause]
I may try to open my eyes, but I will find it impossible to do so.
[Pause]
I stop trying.
[Pause]
I am allowing my whole body to relax including my eyes.

[Pause]

Relax, relax my eyelids now, my eyelids are no longer sealed together, and they are no longer heavy, but I will keep my eyes closed until I am told to open them.

I am going to relax my body, and as I relax my body, I will go deeper and deeper into hypnosis.

When I am told to I will take a deep breath and hold it for a count of seven.

As I exhale, I will say to myself or aloud: 'Relax, relax, relax.'

Each time I say the word 'relax' to myself three times successively, I will immediately feel all my stress and worries flow out of my body, from the top of my head out through my feet.

[Pause]

I will take a deep breath now.

Exhale — Relax, Relax, Relax

[COUNT FROM ONE TO SEVEN] 1-2-3-4-5-6-7

[Repeat four times.]

I am going to relax my body from the bottom of my feet to the top of my head, and as I relax I am going deeper and deeper, and deeper into a relaxed hypnotic sleep.

I will listen only to my voice. I will concentrate on what I am saying.

I am going to start with my left foot.

Relax all of the muscles around my foot, my toes, the bottom of my foot, and the top of my foot.

[Pause]

I am now moving my attention from my foot up my left leg to the top of my thigh.

I am relaxing all of my muscles, the large ones and the small ones, and as I do so I am going deeper and deeper into a relaxed hypnotic sleep.

I am relaxing all of my muscles, the large ones and the small ones, and as I do so I am going deeper and deeper into a relaxed hypnotic sleep.

[Pause]

I am now relaxing my right foot.

I am relaxing all of the muscles in my right foot, my toes, the bottom of my foot and the top of my foot.

Relax, relax, relax.

[Pause]

I am relaxing all of the muscles from the bottom of my right foot all the way up to the top of my thigh.

Relaxing the big muscles and the little muscles.

[Pause]

Both of my legs are totally and completely relaxed from the bottom of my feet to the top of my thighs, and I am going deeper and deeper and deeper into a relaxed hypnotic state.

My pelvic area is relaxed.

[Pause]

I am moving my attention up my body, relaxing my lower tummy, and upper tummy.

[Pause]

I am relaxing my lower chest area, breast muscles, and upper chest area, all the way to the top of my shoulders.

[Pause]

My buttocks muscles are relaxed.

[Pause]

Now I will move my attention up my spinal column all the way up to the top of my back.

I am letting all the tension and stress flow from the center of my spinal column outward from my spinal column to my sides, as I move my attention up to the top of my shoulders.

Relax, relax, relax.

[Pause]

I am relaxing my left arm all the way up to the top of my shoulders. I am now completely relaxed from the top of my shoulders to the bottom of my feet, and I am going deeper and deeper and deeper into a relaxed hypnotic sleep.

[Pause]

I am relaxing my neck muscles, and the muscles on the back, sides, and top of my head.

[Pause]

I am relaxing my facial muscles, including my eyes.

Relax, relax, relax.

[Pause]

I am relaxing my left hand and arm all the way up to the top of my shoulders.

I am completely relaxed from the top of my shoulders to the bottom of my feet, and I am going deeper and deeper and deeper into a relaxed hypnotic sleep.

[Pause]

My neck muscles, including my eyes are relaxed.

[Pause]

My entire body is now relaxed, and I feel fantastic.

Whenever I say the words

'SLEEP, SLEEP, SLEEP.'

I will instantly be in a deep relaxed hypnotic sleep and every time I say the words

'SLEEP, SLEEP, SLEEP'

I will go deeper and faster into this relaxed hypnotic sleep.

I will listen only to my voice now. I will concentrate on what I am saying.

I will take a deep breath NOW,

I will take a deep breath and hold it to the coumt of seven NOW, [COUNT FROM ONE TO SEVEN] 1-2-3-4-5-6-7
Exhale – Relax, Relax, Relax.
I am now completely relaxed and I am thinking of something very pleasant.
Something that I really like to do. Do so now.
[Pause for 30 seconds]
Come back to my voice.
SLEEP, SLEEP, SLEEP.
Whenever I say the word 'sleep' three times successively, I will instantly go into a deep, relaxed, hypnotic sleep.
I will straighten out my left hand and arm now. I am tightening the muscles in my left hand and arm. They are becoming stiff and straight as a steel bar. As I do this, my left hand and arm are becoming heavier and heavier.
I cannot raise my left hand and arm. The harder I try, the heavier my hand and arm become. It's as if lead weights are being added to my hand and arm, pulling it down, down, down.
I may try to raise my hand and arm now, but I cannot do so.
[Pause]
Stop trying,
Relax my left hand and arm completely.
My left hand and arm are no longer heavy. All the weight has been removed.
My hand and arm are totally relaxed and are now flexible, not stiff and straight.
My hand and arm have returned to normal.
I feel fabulous. I am very happy and relaxed and deep, deep, deep into hypnosis.
I am going to count backwards from twenty to one and as I do so I will go deeper and deeper and deeper into hypnosis.

I am going to count backwards from twenty to one and as I do so I will go deeper and deeper and deeper into hypnosis.
I will float very softly as I count downward.
[COUNT FROM TWENTY TO ONE] 20-19-18-17-16-15-14-13-12-11-10-9-8-7-6-5-4-3-2-1
I am now deep, deep, deep into a relaxed hypnotic sleep.
SLEEP, SLEEP, SLEEP.
Come back to my voice now.
My voice is very relaxing and soothing, and as I talk I am going deeper and deeper into hypnosis.
[Pause]
Not now, but when I say to do so, I will visualize the number one goal I want to achieve. When I do so I will picture it as if it's already completed. I will also use all applicable senses when I visualize this goal. For example, my sense of sight ... smell ... taste ... touch, and sound. I can even use my emotions. I will visualixe my achieved goal now.
[30 second Pause]
Come back to my voice. I am very happy and relaxed and I enjoy setting and achieving goals. I will find it easy to do so and I will work on my goals on a daily basis. I am a good person. I am intelligent, organized and loved. I smile a lot and am very happy. I will achieve all of my goals. I will find it easier and easier to do so.
SLEEP SLEEP SLEEP
In a moment I will visualize myself as already having achieved goal number two. I will use all of my senses including sight ... smell ... taste ... touch ... sound, and emotions. I will visualize my second completed goal NOW.
[30 second Pause]
Come back to my voice. I am very hapy, very relaxed and I'm

going DEEPER, DEEPER, AND DEEPER into a relaxed hypnotic state as I talk. SLEEP SLEEP SLEEP
I'm going to take a deep breath and hold it while I count to 7. As I exhale I'll say the words 'RELAX RELAX RELAX'. All worries and stress immediately flow from the top of my head to the tip of my toes and out of my body. Take a deep breath NOW .... 1..2..3..4..5..6..7 EXHALE.
RELAX RELAX RELAX all worry and stress flow instantly out of my body and I'm very happy and relaxed.
Take another deep breath NOW. 1..2..3..4..5..6..7 EXHALE.
RELAX RELAX RELAX
All worries and stress flow instantly out of my body. I feel great.
One more time. Take a deep breath NOW. 1..2..3..4..5..6..7..
EXHALE. RELAX RELAX RELAX
All worries and stress have left my body and I feel relaxed and happy. I am very happy.
Every single day I will state positive affirmations to myself, silently or aloud. I'll feel them flow through my body. Some possibilities include:
EVERY DAY IN EVERY WAY I AM BETTER AND BETTER.
[3 second Pause]
EVERY DAY IN EVERY WAY I AM BETTER AND BETTER.
[3 second Pause]
EVERY DAY IN EVERY WAY I AM BETTER AND BETTER.
[3 second Pause]
I am totally relaxed now, feeling very happy. Now I'm going to go back in time to a place where I am very happy. It could be a birthday, holiday, or some other happy occasion. When I am there, I will use all of my senses that apply: sight ... sound ... taste ... sound ... touch, and emotions. I am in that happy place NOW.
[90 second Pause]

Come back to my voice. I am very happy and relaxed. I will not awaken until I say to do so, then I will awaken quietly, quickly and easily. I will feel totally at ease and relaxed and very happy. SLEEP ... SLEEP ... SLEEP ... DEEPER ... AND DEEPER ... AND DEEPER.

When I say to do so, I will visualize as having already achieved goal number three. I will use all of my senses that apply: Sight ... smell ... taste ... touch ... sound ... and my emotions.

I will visualize my third goal NOW.

[90 second Pause]

Come back to my voice. I enjoy using this tape and setting and achieving my goals. The more I listen to this tape, the more it can help me to achieve all of my dreams and desires. I am a good person. I am intelligent. I have drive and ambition and I know that I am a winner.

I am NOW going to count from one to five. Once I reach the number five, I will be wide awake and feeling wonderful. I will have a great day today.

One ... I am starting to wake up.

Two ... I am waking up further.

Three ... My eyes are beginning to open.

Four ... My eyes are opening and I am waking up more and more.

Five ... My eyes are open and I am wide awake and feeling wonderful.

[Give a great big stretch.]

I am wide awake now and feeling wonderful.

STRESS REDUCTION AND SLEEP HYPNOSIS

This tape is about difficulty sleeping due to stress. Simply using any one of my hypnosis tapes will help you sleep better and will help reduce stress. In the short term stress can be helpful, but over time it becomes destructive.

To decrease stress:

1. Be physically active at least 30 minutes per day, but avoid working out three hours prior to going to bed. Physical activity releases tension and normalizes stress hormones.

2. Break the stress cycle with daily relaxation.
Take frequent breaks throughout the day: stretch, get a drink, take a brief walk, practice deep breathing, take a one minute vacation or take a hot bath.

3. Get adequate rest.

4. Do something you enjoy each day.

5. Develop supportive relationships.

6. Enjoy a massage.

To sleep better:

1. Develop a sleep schedule and stick to it.

2. Avoid caffeine, nicotine, and alcohol, especially just prior to going to bed.

3. Engage in relaxing activities before bed. Reading and soaking in a hot tub are a few possibilities.

4. Create a cozy sleep environment, wear comfortable pajamas, keep the temperature of the room comfortable, darken the room, and use soft comfortable bedding.

5. If, after going to bed your mind is still agitated, get out of bed for a few minutes and do something relaxing, like read.

This tape is to be used when you are ready to go to sleep.

At the end of this tape you will drift off into peaceful sleep.

Stress Reduction and Sleep Hypnosis Tape

Give good lead time (20 seconds).

I am becoming more and more relaxed as I talk.
I am concentrating on what I am saying,
I will listen only to my voice.
My eyelids are getting heavier and heavier, heavier, and heavier.
[Pause]
I feel like lead weights are being put on my eyelids and pulling them down, down, down.
[Pause]
Heavier and heavier, and heavier.
My eyelids are so heavy they are starting to close.
I cannot keep them open.
I may close my eyes any time I want to.
They are getting heavier and heavier and heavier.
My eyelids are closing, closing, closing.
If I have not already done so I am closing my eyes now.
My eyelids are sealed together tight, tight, tight, just as if they were glued or zipped closed.
[Pause]
I cannot open my eyes. The harder I try the tighter my eyes become sealed together.
[Pause]
I may try to open my eyes, but I will find it impossible to do so.
[Pause]
I stop trying.
[Pause]
My whole body including my eyes is relaxing.
[Pause]

My eyelids are relaxing now, my eyelids are no longer sealed together, and they are no longer heavy, but I will keep my eyes closed until I am told to open them.
My body is relaxing, and as my body relaxes, I will go deeper and deeper into hypnosis.
When I am told to I will take a deep breath and hold it for a count of seven,
As I exhale, I will say the words to myself or aloud:
Relax, Relax, Relax.
Any time I say the word 'relax' three times successively I will immediately feel all my stress and worries flow out of my body, from the top of my head out through my feet.
All of my cares and worries will be gone and I feel very happy and content.
[Pause]
I will take a deep breath now.
[COUNT FROM ONE TO SEVEN] 1-2-3-4-5-6-7
Exhale—Relax, Relax, Relax
[Repeat this four times]
My body is relaxing from the bottom of my feet to the top of my head, and as I relax I am going deeper and deeper and deeper into a relaxed hypnotic sleep.
I will listen only to my voice. I will concentrate on what I am saying.
I am going to start with my left foot, relaxing all of the muscles around my foot, my toes, the bottom of my foot, and the top of my foot.
[Pause]
My buttocks muscles are relaxed.
[Pause]
Now I will move my attention up my spinal column all the way up

to the top of my back.
I am letting all the tension and stress flow from the center of my spinal column outward from my spinal column to my sides, as I move my attention up to the top of my shoulders.
Relax, relax, relax.
[Pause]
I am relaxing my left hand and arm all the way up to the top of my shoulders.
All of the big muscles and little muscles.
[Pause]
I am relaxing my right hand and arm all the way to the top of my shoulders.
I am now completely relaxed from the top of my shoulders to the bottom of my feet, and I am going deeper and deeper and deeper into a relaxed hypnotic sleep.
[Pause]
I am relaxing my neck muscles, and the muscles on the back, sides, and top of my head.
I am relaxing my facial muscles, including my eyes.
[Pause]
My entire body is now relaxed and I feel fantastic. When I am told to do so, I will take a deep breath and hold it for a count of seven. Once I release it I will be deeply, deeply, relaxed in a hypnotic sleep. Whenever I say the words,
'SLEEP, SLEEP, SLEEP,'
I will instantly be in a deep relaxed hypnotic sleep and every time I say the words
'SLEEP, SLEEP, SLEEP,'
I will go deeper and faster into this relaxing hypnotic sleep.
I will listen only to my voice now. I will concentrate on what I am saying.

I will take a deep breath and hold it to the count of seven NOW,
[COUNT ONE TO SEVEN] 1-2-3-4-5-6-7
Exhale—Relax, relax, relax.
[Repeat four times.]
I am now completely relaxed and I want to think of something very pleasant.
Something that I really like to do.
[Pause 30 seconds]
Come back to my voice now.
SLEEP, SLEEP, SLEEP
Whenever I say the word sleep three times successively I will instantly go into a deep relaxed hypnotic sleep.
I will straighten out my left hand and arm now. I am tightening the muscles in my left hand and arm. They are becoming stiff and straight as a steel bar. As I do this my left hand and arm are becoming heavier and heavier.
I cannot raise my left hand and arm. The harder I try, the heavier my hand and arm become. It's as if lead weights are being added to my hand and arm, pulling it down, down, down.
I may try to raise my hand and arm now, but I cannot do so.
[Pause]
I stop trying.
I relax my left hand and arm completely.
My left hand and arm are no longer heavy, all the weight has been removed.
My hand and arm are totally relaxed and are now flexible, not stiff and straight.
My hand and arm have returned to normal.
I feel fabulous. I am very happy and relaxed and deep, deep, deep into hypnosis.

I am going to count backwards from twenty to one and as I do so I will go deeper and deeper and deeper into hypnosis.
I will float very softly as I count downward.
[COUNT FROM TWENTY TO ONE] 20-19-18-17-16-15-14-13-12-11-10-9-8-7-6-5-4-3-2-1.
I am now deep, deep, deep, into a relaxed hypnotic sleep.
SLEEP, SLEEP, SLEEP.
Come back to my voice now.
My voice is very relaxing and soothing. As I listen to my voice, I go deeper and deeper into hypnosis.
[Pause]
Any time I feel myself getting stressed or find myself in a stressful situation, I will simply take a deep breath then exhale saying to myself or aloud the words,
'RELAX, RELAX, RELAX'
I will be instantly relaxed and at ease. All worry and stress will instantly leave my mind and body and I will be left with a happy content feeling.
I control my own life and I control the amount of stress that enters my mind, because I control my thoughts.
I now visualize something that is a constant source of stress.
[Pause 6 seconds]
Now I picture myself calming down, I am not going to allow this to stress me out any more. I will say the word 'relax' to myself three times.
RELAX, RELAX, RELAX.
[Pause]
I am calm now.
Whenever I am ready to go to sleep, I will find that I do so easily, comfortably and quickly.
I will think relaxed thoughts and drift into a nice, peaceful sleep.

I will have wonderful dreams and will wake up in the morning feeling energized and full of life, very upbeat and happy. I will find that this comes to me more and more easily as I listen to this tape.
I visualize myself sleeping peacefully.
[Pause 6 seconds]
Come back to my voice.
I enjoy using this tape and I will do so often.
The more I listen to this tape, the more it will help me achieve a great night's sleep and reduce stress from my life.
I am a good person. I am intelligent. I have drive and ambition, and I know that I am a winner.
I am now going into a deep relaxed sleep.
I feel comfortable and relaxed.
I will awaken in the morning feeling wonderful and looking forward to the day.
[End tape]

Non-Smoking Hypnosis Tape

Give good lead time (20 seconds.)
NOTE: If you want to stop without cutting back, modify. Just state: I am now a non-smoker.

I am becoming more relaxed as I talk.
I am concentrating on what I am saying,
I will listen only to my voice.
My eyelids are getting heavier and heavier, heavier, and heavier.
[Pause]
I feel like lead weights are being put on my eyelids and pulling them down, down, down.
[Pause]
Heavier and heavier, and heavier.
My eyelids are so heavy they are starting to close. I cannot keep them open. I may close my eyes any time I want to.
They are getting heavier and heavier and heavier,
My eyelids are closing, closing, closing.
If I have not already done so, I will close my eyes now.
My eyelids are sealed tight, tight, tight, together.
I will visualize my eyelids sealed together, just as if they were glued or zipped closed.
[Pause]
I cannot open my eyes. The harder I try the tighter my eyes become sealed together.
[Pause]
I may try to open my eyes, but I will find it impossible to do so.
[Pause]
I stop trying.
[Pause]

I will allow my whole body to relax including my eyes.

[Pause]

RELAX, RELAX, my eyelids.

Now, my eyelids are no longer sealed together, and they are no longer heavy, but I will keep my eyes closed until I am told to open them.

I am going to relax my body, and as I relax my body, I will go deeper and deeper into hypnosis.

When I am told to I will take a deep breath and hold it for a count of seven. As I exhale, I will say to myself or aloud,

'RELAX, RELAX, RELAX.'

Any time I say the word 'relax' to myself three times successively, I will immediately feel all my stress and worries flow out of my body, from the top of my head out through my feet.

[Pause]

I will take a deep breath now.

[COUNT FROM SEVEN TO ONE] 7-6-5-4-3-2-1

Exhale- Relax, Relax, Relax

[Repeat this four times]

I am going to relax my body from the bottom of my feet to the top of my head, and as I relax I'm going deeper and deeper and deeper into a relaxed hypnotic sleep.

I will listen only to my voice. I will concentrate on what I am saying.

I am going to start with my left foot, relax all of the muscles around my foot, my toes, the bottom of my foot, and the top of my foot.

[Pause]

Now I will move my attention from my foot up my left leg to the top of my thigh.

Relax all of the muscles, the large ones and the small ones, and as I do so I am going deeper and deeper into a relaxed hypnotic sleep.

[Pause]

Now I'll relax my right foot.

I am relaxing all of the muscles in my right foot, my toes, the bottom of my foot and the top of my foot.

RELAX, RELAX, RELAX.

[Pause]

I am relaxing all of the muscles from the bottom of my right foot all the way up to the top of my thigh.

I am relaxing the big muscles and the little muscles.

[Pause]

Both of my legs are totally and completely relaxed from the bottom of my feet to the top of my thighs, and I am going deeper and deeper and deeper into a relaxed hypnotic state.

My pelvic area is relaxed.

[Pause]

I am moving my attention up my body, relaxing my lower tummy, and upper tummy.

[Pause]

I am relaxing my lower chest area, breast muscles, and upper chest area, all the way to the top of my shoulders.

[Pause]

My buttocks muscles are relaxed.

[Pause]

I am moving my attention up my spinal column all the way up to the top of my back.

I let all the tension and stress flow from the center of my spinal column outward from my spinal column to my sides, as I move up to the top of my shoulders.

RELAX, RELAX, RELAX.

[Pause]
I am relaxing my left hand and arm all the way up to the top of my shoulders. All of the big muscles and little muscles.
[Pause]
I am relaxing my right hand and arm all the way to the top of my shoulders. I am now completely relaxed form the top of my shoulders to the bottom of my feet, and I am going deeper and deeper and deeper into a relaxed hypnotic sleep.
[Pause]
My neck muscles and the muscles on the back, sides, and top of my head are relaxed.
[Pause]
My facial muscles, including my eyes, are relaxed.
[Pause]
My entire body is now relaxed and I feel fantastic. When I am told to do so, I will take a deep breath and hold it for a count of seven. Once I release it I will be deeply relaxed in a hypnotic sleep. Whenever I say the words,
'SLEEP, SLEEP, SLEEP.'
I will instantly be in a deep relaxed hypnotic sleep and every time I say the words,
'SLEEP, SLEEP, SLEEP'
I will go deeper and faster into this relaxed hypnotic sleep.
I will listen only to my voice now. I will concentrate on what I am saying.
I will take a deep breath NOW,
[COUNT FROM ONE TO SEVEN] 1-2-3-4-5-6-7
Exhale – Relax, Relax, Relax.
[Repeat four times]
I am now completely relaxed and I will think of something very pleasant.

Something that I really like to do.
[Pause for 30 seconds]
Come back to my voice now.
SLEEP, SLEEP, SLEEP.
Whenever I say the word sleep three times successively, I will instantly go into a deep, relaxed, hypnotic sleep.
I will straighten out my left hand and arm now.
I am tightening the muscles in my left hand and arm. They are becoming stiff and straight as a steel bar. As I do this, my left hand and arm are becoming heavier and heavier.
I cannot raise my left hand and arm. The harder I try, the heavier my hand and arm become. It's as if lead weights are being added to my hand and arm, pulling it down, down, down.
I may try to raise my hand and arm now, but I cannot do so.
[Pause]
I stop trying,
I am relaxing my left hand and arm completely.
My left hand and arm are no longer heavy. All the weight has been removed.
My hand and arm are totally relaxed and are now flexible, not stiff and straight.
My hand and arm have returned to normal. I feel fabulous. I am very happy and relaxed and deep, deep, deep into hypnosis.
I am going to count backwards from twenty to one and as I do so I will go deeper and deeper and deeper into hypnosis.
I will float very softly as I count downward.
[START COUNTING DOWN NOW] 20-19-18-17-16-15-14-13-12-11-10-9-8-7-6-5-4-3-2-1
I am now deep, deep, deep into a relaxed hypnotic sleep.
I will not awaken until I am told to do so. Then I will awaken quickly, quietly, easily, and be completely refreshed and relaxed.

[Pause]

SLEEP, SLEEP, SLEEP.

Now I am going to think about smoking a cigarette, cigar, or pipe, whatever it is I smoke.

I can see it, feel it, taste it and smell it.

I want to quit and I will quit.

I will visualize the following benefits once I have quit.

1. I will breathe more easily.

[Pause]

2. My circulation will improve.

[Pause]

3. I will feel less tired and nervous.

[Pause]

4. My sense of smell will improve.

[Pause]

5. My cough will lessen or disappear entirely.

[Pause]

6. My heart and lungs will strengthen and I will breathe more easily.

[Pause]

7. My sex drive will be enhanced.

[Pause]

8. I will save money.

[Pause]

Once this session is over, I will make a list of all of these benefits, and carry it with me.

I will read this list at least twice a day and visualize all of these benefits to my body and my life.

I will be aware every time I pick up a cigarette, cigar, or pipe, that I am doing so.

I will no longer pick up one of these items without being aware

that I am doing so. My life is so much better now that I have quit smoking.
Whenever I have an urge to pick up a cigarette, I will say the words 'No, no, no,' to myself and the urge will instantly disappear.
I am now visualizing what my life is like smoke-free.
[Pause for 6 seconds]
I will notice the benefits immediately once I quit smoking.
For example:
After eight hours, the nicotine and carbon monoxide levels in my blood will be halved.
After 24 hours carbon monoxide will be eliminated from my body and my lungs will resume their normal cleaning process.
[Pause]
After 48 hours all nicotine will be eliminated from my body.
[Pause]
My sense of taste and smell will begin to improve.
In 72 hours my breathing will improve.
[Pause]
In 2-12 weeks my circulation will improve.
[Pause]
After 3-9 months my lung function will begin to improve decreasing all coughing and breathing problems.
[Pause]
When I am told to do so I will visualize myself smoke-free.
I will use all of my senses to help me achieve this and I will now visualize these benefits.
[Pause 2 minutes]
I enjoy using this tape and I will do so often. The more I listen to this tape the more it will help me to stop smoking, never start again, and improve my health.

[Pause]
I am intelligent.
[Pause]
I have drive and ambition, and I know that I am a winner.
[Pause]
In a minute, I am going to count from one to five. Once I reach the number five, I will be wide awake and feeling wonderful.
I will have a great day today.
One. I am starting to wake up.
Two. I am waking up further.
Three. My eyes are beginning to open.
Four. My eyes are opening, and I am waking up more and more.
Five. My eyes are open and I am wide awake and feeling wonderful.
Stretch in a grand way!
I am wide awake now and feeling wonderful.

Weight Loss Hypnosis Tape

Give good lead time (20 seconds.)

I am becoming more relaxed as I talk.
I am concentrating on what I am saying,
I will listen only to my voice.
My eyelids are getting heavier and heavier, heavier, and heavier.
[Pause]
I feel like lead weights are being put on my eyelids and pulling them down, down, down.
[Pause]
Heavier and heavier, and heavier.
My eyelids are so heavy they are starting to close. I cannot keep them open. I may close my eyes any time I want to.
They are getting heavier and heavier and heavier,
My eyelids are closing, closing, closing.
If I have not already done so, I will close my eyes now.
My eyelids are sealed tight, tight, tight, together.
I will visualize my eyelids sealed together, just as if they were glued or zipped closed.
[Pause]
I cannot open my eyes. The harder I try, the tighter my eyes become sealed together.
[Pause]
I may try to open my eyes, but I will find it impossible to do so.
[Pause]
I stop trying.
[Pause]
I will allow my whole body to relax, including my eyes.
[Pause]

RELAX, RELAX my eyelids.
Now my eyelids are no longer sealed together and they are no longer heavy, but I will keep my eyes closed until I am told to open them.
I am going to relax my body, and as I relax my body, I will go deeper and deeper into hypnosis.
When I am told to, I will take a deep breath and hold it for a count of seven. As I exhale, I will say to myself or aloud, 'RELAX, RELAX, RELAX.'
Any time I say the word 'relax' to myself three times successively. I will immediately feel all my stress and worries flow out of my body, from the top of my head out through my feet.
[Pause]
I will take a deep breath now.
[COUNT BACKWARDS FROM SEVEN TO ONE] 7-6-5-4-3-2-1
Exhale- Relax, Relax, Relax
[Repeat this four times.]
I am going to relax my body from the bottom of my feet to the top of my head, and as I relax I'm going deeper and deeper and deeper into a relaxed hypnotic sleep.
I will listen only to my voice. I will concentrate on what I am saying.
I am relaxing my left foot, relaxing all of the muscles around my foot, my toes, the bottom of my foot, and the top of my foot.
[Pause]
Now I will move my attention from my foot up my left leg to the top of my thigh.
Relax all of the muscles, the large ones and the small ones, and as I do so I am going deeper and deeper into a relaxed hypnotic sleep.
[Pause]

Now I'll relax my right foot.
I am relaxing all of the muscles in my right foot, my toes, the bottom of my foot and the top of my foot.
RELAX, RELAX, RELAX.
[Pause]
I am relaxing all of the muscles from the bottom of my right foot all the way up to the top of my thigh.
Relax the big muscles and the little muscles.
[Pause]
Both of my legs are totally and completely relaxed from the bottom of my feet to the top of my thighs, and I am going deeper and deeper and deeper into a relaxed hypnotic state.
My pelvic area is relaxed.
[Pause]
I am moving my attention up my body, relaxing my lower tummy and upper tummy.
[Pause]
I am relaxing my lower chest area, breast muscles, and upper chest area, all the way to the top of my shoulders.
[Pause]
My buttocks muscles are relaxed.
[Pause]
I am moving my attention up my spinal column all the way up to the top of my back.
I let all the tension and stress flow from the center of my spinal column outward from my spinal column to my sides, as I move up to the top of my shoulders.
RELAX, RELAX, RELAX.
[Pause]
I am relaxing my left hand and arm all the way up to the top of my shoulders. All of the big muscles and little muscles.

[Pause]

I am relaxing my right hand and arm all the way to the top of my shoulders. I am now completely relaxed from the top of my shoulders to the bottom of my feet, and I am going deeper and deeper and deeper and deeper into a relaxed hypnotic sleep.

[Pause]

My neck muscles and the muscles on the back, sides, and top of my head are relaxed.

[Pause]

My facial muscles, including my eyes, are relaxed.

[Pause]

My entire body is now relaxed and I feel fantastic. When I am told to do so, I will take a deep breath and hold it for a count of seven. Once I release it I will be deeply relaxed in a hypnotic sleep. Whenever I say the words,

'SLEEP, SLEEP, SLEEP,'

I will instantly be in a deep relaxed hypnotic sleep and every time I say the words,

'SLEEP, SLEEP, SLEEP'

I will go deeper and faster into this relaxed hypnotic sleep.

I will listen only to my voice now. I will concentrate on what I am saying.

I will take a deep breath NOW,

[COUNT BACKWARDS FROM SEVEN TO ONE] 7-6-5-4-3-2-1

Exhale – Relax, Relax, Relax.

[Repeat four times.]

I am now completely relaxed and I want to think of something very pleasant. Something that I really like to do.

[Pause for 30 seconds.]

Come back to my voice now.

SLEEP, SLEEP, SLEEP.
Whenever I say the word 'sleep' three times successively, I will instantly go into a deep, relaxed, hypnotic sleep.
I will straighten out my left hand and arm now.
I am tightening the muscles in my left hand and arm. They are becoming stiff and straight as a steel bar. As I do this my left hand and arm are becoming heavier and heavier.
I cannot raise my left hand and arm. The harder I try, the heavier my hand and arm become. It's as if lead weights are being added to my hand and arm, pulling it down, down, down.
I may try to raise my hand and arm now, but I cannot do so.
[Pause]
I stop trying,
I will relax my left hand and arm completely.
My left hand and arm are no longer heavy. All the weight has been removed.
My hand and arm are totally relaxed and are now flexible, not stiff and straight.
My hand and arm have returned to normal. I feel fabulous. I am very happy and relaxed and deep, deep, deep into hypnosis.
I am going to count backwards from twenty to one and as I do so I will go deeper and deeper and deeper into hypnosis.
I will float very softly as I count downward.
[START COUNTING DOWN NOW] 20-19-18-17-16-15-14-13-12-11-10-9-8-7-6-5-4-3-2-1
I am now deep, deep, deep into a relaxed hypnotic sleep.
I will not awaken until I am told to do so. Then I will awaken quickly, quietly, easily, and be completely refreshed and relaxed.
[Pause]
SLEEP, SLEEP, SLEEP.
Come back to my voice now.

My voice is very relaxing and soothing, and as I talk I am going deeper and deeper into hypnosis.
[Pause]
I will think of the benefits to my body, self-esteem, and health when I achieve my desired weight.
[Pause 6 seconds.]
I will feel better,
Look better,
And be happier.
[Pause]
When I am told to, I will visualize my body at the ideal weight and shape that I want to be.
I will use all of my senses to do this.
Sight
[Pause]
Smell
[Pause]
Taste
[Pause]
Touch
[Pause]
Sound
[Pause]
I will always do this as if my goal is already achieved.
I will visualize myself in a mirror now.
[Pause]
I look good.
I look at my body from different angles.
[Pause]
My friends and family are telling me how great I look, and I do look great.

I feel my body with my hands, I feel how firm and slim my body is.
I think about my food now.
I will eat smaller, healthier portions of food.
[Pause]
I now taste this healthy food, and it tastes good.
[Pause]
I smell my healthy food.
It smells good.
[Pause]
I will be selective about the food that I eat. Any time that I feel like eating a snack, I will stop and think about it first.
Do I really want or need the snack at that time?
From on I will always be aware of the types of food that I eat and I will make conscious decisions as to whether or not I want to eat those types of food.
[Pause]
I will find that I chew my food slowly before swallowing.
[Pause]
I will limit my food intake at night, and especially after 8:00 p.m.
I will not ride when I can walk.
[Pause]
I will exercise my body at every opportunity.
I will enjoy exercising.
I will find an exercise program that I like and I will do it.
I now visualize an exercise that I like to do.
[Pause for 6 seconds]
I will set a weight goal that I want to achieve and I will set a date when I will finally achieve that goal.
I will weigh myself weekly at approximately the same time and with the same clothing. I will keep a log of my weight loss for

myself.
I will take measurements of my waist, bust, and thighs.
I will do this once a week when I weigh myself.
I will write down the ideal inches that I will be and the dates that I will reach those goals.
I will keep a log of the inches that I lose.
Come back to my voice.
I enjoy using this tape and setting and achieving my weight goals.
I will listen to this tape often.
The more I listen to this tape, the more it will help me to achieve all of my dreams and desires.
I am a good person.
[Pause]
I am intelligent.
[Pause]
I have drive and ambition, and I know that I am a winner.
[Pause]
In a minute, I am going to count from one to five. Once I reach the number five, I will be wide awake and feeling wonderful.
I will have a great day today.
One. I am starting to wake up.
Two. I am waking up further.
Three. My eyes are beginning to open.
Four. My eyes are opening, and I am waking up more and more.
Five. My eyes are open and I am wide awake and feeling wonderful.
Stretch in a grand way!
I am wide awake now and feeling wonderful.

CHAPTER 8

AFFIRMATIONS

Nothing in this World is more important than a healthy state of mind. With that, all things are possible. A healthy state of mind complements any life situation.

Affirmations are a powerful way for conditioning the mind to maintain optimum health throughout our entire life. They are practiced by writing them out, saying them aloud to ourselves, rehearsing them privately in our minds, and recording them and playing them back.

I have listed some positive affirmations you can use to help you achieve success in any area. Pick those which feel best for you and then personalize them to fit you. Those selected should evoke significant emotional responses from you.

Once you have selected one or two you like, write and post them where you will see them daily. You need to repeat your positive affirmation aloud or to yourself throughout the day and with feeling. The more emotion you put into stating your affirmations, the quicker you will obtain results.

Repeat these affirmations for at least thirty days. This will settle them in your subconscious mind.

Here are a few more guidelines for practicing Affirmations:

• Affirm that something is happening *here* and *now*. Be careful that you are not affirming something *will* happen *in the future*. This is actually a negative affirmation because it says, "Oh, *someday* I will be rich." Place results in *today*, rather than the future.

• Affirm only the desired result, without placing any hidden reference to undesired things. For example: Affirm, "My relationship is healthy and loving," rather than affirming, "My boring relationship is getting better." Affirm what you want, rather than what you want to get rid of.

• Use the first person and include your full name in every affirmation sentence. Example: "I, Ronald G. Miller, am a happy, healthy, wholesome person."

• Practice only one or two affirmations at a time, giving them the time to work on the subconscious before moving on to other affirmations. Affirmations are like planting seeds. Nourish them with continued energy every day. Give them time to work and sprout results. Be open to creative ways that affirmations manifest results.

• Affirmations are practiced by repetition and are done every day. Repetition produces results, excuses don't. Write them out ten or twenty times each morning and each evening. Record and play them back while exercising, working, and/or driving. Paste them on notes around your house. Rehearse them in your mind when challenged by a difficult situation. *Cultivate What You Want To Grow.*

• Positive mind conditioning can cause all sorts of hidden subconscious material to surface. If you begin to experience negative feelings or stubborn negative thoughts, it means the affirmations are producing results and shaking loose subconscious material. Work with these reactions by ventilating with a trusted person, writing in a personal journal, or seeking guidance.

Affirmations for Getting Started

- I have a basic Trust that my Affirmations will work and my Efforts will be rewarded.
- My mind is constantly creating Optimistic and Positive thoughts about everything I do.
- I was born with a Limitless Capacity for Wellness and Growth.
- I like myself, because I know my Identity and Uniqueness.
- I am One Hundred Percent alive because I think, speak, and act Enthusiastically.
- I bring great Concentration to bear upon any subject at any time.
- I am Efficient in everything that I do.
- I face problems with Courage, and thus Solve any and all problems easily.
- I have a completely relaxed Self-Assurance, and I am sure of myself in all situations and with all people.
- I Persevere and I Finish any task that I undertake.
- I am Honest with myself, and with everyone else.
- I treat all problems as opportunities to be Creative, knowing that my qualities of Leadership are Determined by the Creativity I use in every part of my life.
- I possess an Abundant supply of Energy and draw upon it at will.
- I am Well-Organized in every phase of my life.
- I have a Fantastic Memory. It grows better and better every day.
- I am an Enthusiastic Speaker; Well Prepared, Logical, and Sincere before any group.

- I read quickly and easily with great Comprehension of all subject matter.
- I contact, feel, and easily show my Emotions to myself and to all other people.
- I Relax as deeply as I wish at any time I want.
- I am quickly and accurately Decisive in all matters.
- I do everything Right Now as it needs doing.
- Because of my great Warmth, Self-Assurance, Enthusiasm, and Knowledge, I am a success, motivating other people to accomplish their best.
- I Expect good things to happen to me today.
- I am OK because I am on my way to success.

Affirmations for Prosperity

- I am powerfully positive in everything I think, do, and say.
- I have an ever-renewing storehouse of energy every day in my life.
- Because I am so thorough and skilled in my work, the universe is constantly rewarding me.
- The universe is generous and gives me everything I need every day.
- I am extremely rich in blessings, intelligence, character, wisdom, skills, and insight.
- I already possess within me anything I need to become anything I want to be.
- Money comes to me easily and abundantly.
- I am very prosperous in all my business dealings.
- I am positive and prosperous in everything I do every day.
- I interact easily and positively with all other people; therefore, people love doing business with me.

- Because of my qualities, people are positively attracted to me as a businessperson.
- People seek me out to do business with me because they like my qualities.
- I perform work tasks with great skill and friendliness; therefore, people come to me for opportunities.
- Prosperity is always working to find ways of expressing itself in my life.
- My prosperity shines in my personality, and others enjoy being with me.
- I possess an endless supply of creativity, energy, and tolerance for any work or project that I assume.
- Prosperous people are attracted to me.
- I have abundant qualities that always propel me toward prosperity.
- As prosperity in everything I think, do, and say is constantly created, the world becomes a playground and I have heartfelt fun every day.

Affirmations for Work

- The Universe freely hands me work that I love to do.
- I do all my work with a free spirit and unlimited creativity.
- I always have a great source of energy for my work, because I am doing work that I love to do.
- I have everything I need to perform all the work tasks in front of me.
- I have just the right amount of time to easily and comfortably do all my jobs.
- I see all my work as opportunity to express myself, and to develop to greater levels of achievement.

- Because I am sincere and honest at any job I do, my efforts always bring accomplishment and monetary reward.
- Work is not just to make money, but it is my opportunity every day to become a more accomplished, more aware, wiser person.
- Because I am efficient, thoughtful, creative, wise, and skilled in any work that I do, I always feel respect from people working with me.
- My work and skill bring money for my needs. My love of what I do brings me success.
- I am very fortunate to be able to work at what I love to do.
- Much of the work that I do in this world for pay is something that I would be doing anyway, even if I were not paid.
- The Universe is always seeking opportunities for me to move in new and wonderful areas of work and advancement.
- Everything I do turns into success.
- Because everything I do turns into success, people really love working with me and around me.
- I am the kind of person that other people love to work around and to have as a work partner.
- I attract to myself, other positive-minded people who also have steady and sure success in all their works.
- Any work before me is a golden opportunity to learn, explore, develop, understand, contribute, achieve, build, promote, help, and become anything I desire.
- I am fearless in the face of deadlines or hard work.
- A deep storehouse of extremely positive thinking manifests within me in any situation of need.
- My success is contagious, other people like it, other people seek it, and other people respect it.

Affirmations for Relationships

- I am positive, secure and confident in myself: therefore, positive, secure, confident people are attracted to me every day.
- I know clearly who I am and what I want in personal relationships.
- I attract powerfully positive and healthy people into my life.
- I am caring, wise, supportive and fun to be with.
- I feel completely at ease and comfortable with all people.
- I am a winner in all my relationships.
- I make valuable contributions in my relationships every day.
- I have a rich collection of friends who value my qualities.
- I experience all my personal relationships with great consciousness.
- I am always being guided in my personal relationships by a powerful and wise inner spiritual self.
- I am powerfully and intuitively guided with any changes in my personal relationships.
- Growth and change in my intimate love relationships is always directed toward good.
- I am wise, honest, thoughtful, and healthy in my love relationships, and others treat me the same.
- I experience love deeply and grow richer because of this every day.
- I am extremely successful in my love relationships.
- I am a sensual, thoughtful, passionate lover, and my partner's are sensual, thoughtful, and passionate in their love for me.
- I am a fully alive human being with an ever-renewing trust for love in my life.
- All my desires in relationships are being fulfilled every day.
- I possess complete ability to express my feelings, intentions, and thoughts in all my relationships and I express myself wisely.

- Because I am completely confident in my health, honesty, and inner wisdom, I invest in personal relationships knowing deeply that I can deal with anything I may need to.
- I know only love and have completely forgotten how to be afraid in any of my relationships.
- I always do the healthy thing in my relationships.

Affirmations for Wounds

- I am a child of God.
- I deserve to be loved by myself and others.
- I am whole and good.
- I deserve love, peace, prosperity, and serenity.
- I am a precious person.
- I forgive myself for having let others hurt me.
- I am capable of changing.
- I forgive myself for hurting myself and others.
- I am a worthwhile person.
- I forgive myself for accepting sex when I wanted love.
- I am willing to accept love.
- Just for today I will be vulnerable with someone I trust.
- I am not alone; I am one with God and the Universe.
- I have ample leisure time without feeling guilty.
- Just for today I will respect my own boundaries and the boundaries of others.
- Just for today I will take a compliment and hold it in my heart for more than just a fleeting moment. I will let it nurture me.
- The pain that I might feel by remembering can't be any worse than the pain I feel by knowing and not remembering.
- The more I like myself the more others like themselves.
- I am a happy, healthy, wholesome, beautiful, positive, prosper-

ous person.

- I am a unique and priceless person, coming from a unique and perfect pattern within me.
- I am an extremely well-liked and pleasing person.
- I am extremely successful in everything I do and say.
- I am a self-determined person, and I allow others the same right.
- I can say 'No' to other people and know I remain loved and cared for.
- Other people have the right to say 'No' to me and I know that we still love and care for each other.
- I have the right and responsibility to express my anger and remain loved and I take responsibility to clean up any mess and restore harmony when appropriate.
- I love myself unconditionally just as I am.

Affirmations for Love

- I love myself completely.
- I have unconditional and abundant love within me.
- Love comes to me easily and naturally.
- I give and receive love easily and joyfully.
- My life is filled with loving people who care about me and support me.
- Others love me easily and joyfully.
- I now feel loved and appreciated by my parents, my friends, and everyone who is important to me.
- I always have an abundant supply of love within me.
- I give freely from my endless inner supply of love.
- I always deserve love from myself and others.
- I have a strong and unfailing center of self-love inside of me.

- I have a strong and unfailing center of love and compassion for others inside of me.
- I feel wonderful when I express the limitless love and compassion inside of me.
- I express my love freely, knowing that, as I give away love, I am instantly supplied with more.
- I am passionately and lovingly interested in everyone.
- I radiate love to all persons and places and things that I contact each day.
- People are just waiting to love me and I let them love me abundantly.
- I am a free channel through which love always flows into expression, and nothing exists inside of me to block this endless flow of love.
- I breathe in universal love and it radiates through every cell in my body.
- Love flows through me to all humanity.
- I attract loving, beautiful people into my life.
- I am abundant with love and happiness, and I rejoice in the happiness of others.
- Everyone who touches me from near or far is now receiving perfect love.
- My love is instantly transmitted to the subconscious of other people around me.
- Love rules my consciousness and guides me through my every step, every day.
- Nothing exists within my consciousness except perfect love.
- The love inside of me forgives everything.
- I have love inside of me as my natural birthright. It is inside of me as standard equipment. There is nothing I need to do to acquire love. It is already inside of me.

- I always deserve love. I deserve love just for being alive.

General Affirmations

- I give myself all the permission I need to do what I know is best.
- I trust and rely upon my excellent sense of judgement in every thing I do.
- I am the best judge of what is best for me, and I trust my judgement completely.
- I have complete and unconditional worth as a person in this universe.
- I am fully competent and capable in everything that I decide to do.
- All of my accomplishments are because I am a fully functioning, capable, competent human being.
- My worth as a human being is unconditional, and other people unconditionally like me.
- I am respected and well-liked by all people that I know.
- I accept and acknowledge unconditionally my individuality and unique personality.
- I respect myself, I respect all other persons, and all other people respect me.
- I can trust myself completely as my life unfolds to create my own unique story
- I am highly creative, intelligent, attractive, energetic, sexy, witty, smart, healthy, wealthy, and wise.

CHAPTER 9

RECOMMENDED RESOURCES

These are some of the many books that I have read and recommend.

1. *Think and Grow Rich* by Napoleon Hill

2. *The Power of Positive Thinking* by Norman Vincent Peale

3. *How to Win Friends and Influence People* by Dale Carnegie

4. *Mission Success* by Og Mandino

5. *Move Ahead With Possibility Thinking* by Robert H. Schuller

6. *Discover Your Possibilities* by Robert H. Schuller

7. *The Million Dollar Secret Hidden in Your Mind* by Anthony Norvell

8. *Don't Worry, Make Money* by Richard Carlson Ph.D.

9. *The Magic of Believing* by Claude M. Bristol

10. *Dare to Win* by Jack Canfield and Mark Victor Hansen

11. *The Procrastinator's Handbook- Mastering the Art of Doing It Now* by Rita Emmet

CONCLUSION

This is the first day of the rest of my life.

I hope you have enjoyed our short time together, but even more than that, I hope I have given you some information that will change the direction of your life for the better. I know it won't be easy to return to your busy schedule and maintain the goals that you have decided are important to you. Please remember the goals that you have selected are your goals, nobody else's, and you are worthy of their achievement. Sure, it will take work and juggling of schedules. Just remember: "IT WORKS"!

POSSIBILITY THINKERS CREED

Robert Schuller, Crystal Cathedral, California

When faced with a mountain
I will not quit!
I will keep on striving
Until I climb over,
Find a pass through,
Tunnel underneath,
Or simply stay…
And turn the mountain
Into a gold mine,
With God's help.

ABOUT THE AUTHOR

RONALD G. MILLER is a dynamic speaker in goal setting, stress reduction, positive thinking, real estate, and finances. He has spoken before groups such as the American Lung Association, Galen Club, Apartment owners associations, real estate boards, the Elks and Kiwanis Clubs, and many other institutions and clubs. Mr. Miller is a member of the Arizona Club, Phoenix, AZ and the Phoenix and Scottsdale Chambers of Commerce. He is a member of the National Guild of Hypnotists and is a Certified Hypnotherapist.

A nationally known expert on real estate and financial planning, Mr. Miller has been published in the International Association of Financial Planners, Millionaires Manual, and numerous real estate magazines. He has also been a guest speaker on several talk shows. Having held both Real Estate and Insurance brokers licenses in Nevada and California, Mr. Miller was also the successful owner and CEO of two financial planning firms, two mortgage companies, two real estate companies, and two tax and accounting companies in California and Nevada.

Ronald Miller was born and raised in Maine and currently resides in Phoenix, AZ. He graduated Magna Cum Laude. He was in the United States Marines, serving one hitch in Vietnam and receiving an honorable discharge.

Mr. Miller began researching and studying hypnosis, goal setting and positive thinking in the late 1960's. Since then he has presented hundreds of seminars, lectures and classes covering a variety of topics such as: financial planning, estate planning, real estate-buying, selling, and financing, goal setting, and stress reduction. He has helped many individuals stop smoking, lose weight, decrease stress, and achieve their goals.

Ronald Miller developed *IT WORKS* to help others discover their dreams and make them realities. The *IT WORKS* book, seminar and workbooks help create a dynamic model focused on helping individuals accomplish what they truly want in life without letting fear and failure get in their way.

Find out more about IT WORKS tapes and seminars:

IT WORKS

3104 E. Camelback Road #159, Phoenix, AZ 85016

Phone: 602-248-0078

Fax: 602-212-0880

Email: info@itworksinfinitely.com

www.itworksinfinitely.com